Also from Westphalia Press
westphaliapress.org

Saber & Scroll

Volume 3
Issue 2
Spring-Summer
2014

Editor-in-Chief,
Anne Midgley

WESTPHALIA PRESS
An imprint of Policy Studies Organization

Saber & Scroll: Volume 3, Issue 2, Spr/Sum 2014

Westphalia Press
An imprint of Policy Studies Organization
1527 New Hampshire Ave., NW
Washington, D.C. 20036
info@ipsonet.org

ISBN-13: 978-1-63391-881-8
ISBN-10: 1-63391-881-5

Cover design by Jeffrey Barnes:
jbarnesbook.design

Daniel Gutierrez-Sandoval, Executive Director
PSO and Westphalia Press

Updated material and comments on this edition
can be found at the Westphalia Press website:
www.westphaliapress.org

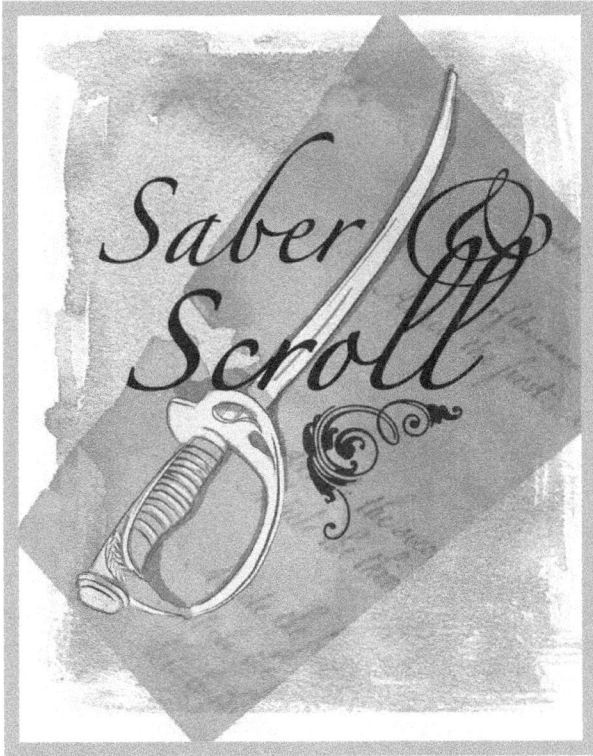

Saber and Scroll Journal

Volume III Issue II

Spring-Summer 2014

Saber and Scroll Historical Society

1

Logo Design: Julian Maxwell

Cover Design: DeAnna Stevens

Cover Image: Macrovector/shutterstock.com

Members of the Saber and Scroll Historical Society, the volunteer staff at the Saber and Scroll Journal publishes quarterly.

saberandscroll.weebly.com

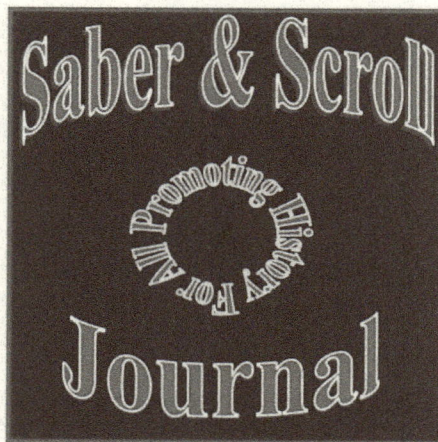

Journal Staff

Editor-In-Chief
Anne Midgley

Content Editors
Chris Booth, Joe Cook, Mike Gottert, Rebecca Simmons Graf,
Kathleen Guler, Michael Majerczyk, Matt Meador, Anne Midgley,
William Potter, Ben Sorenson, Melanie Thornton, Chris Schloemer,
Kay O'Pry-Reynolds

Copy Editors
DeAnna Stevens

Proofreaders
Aida Dias, Frank Hoeflinger, Lew Taylor, Susanne Watts

Webmaster
Danielle Crooks

Contents

From The Editor   5

Henry Clay is Dead: The End of Compromise in   6
Antebellum America

Joseph Cook

Τύχη: Fortune, Fate and Chance in Herodotus and Thucydides   23

Benjamin Sorensen

The Conscience of a Nation: The Social Work of Jane Addams
In Chicago's Immigrant Communities   42

Susanne Watts

Conquerors and Conquered: Early Perspectives of the
Battle of Hastings   55

Matthew Hudson

The Ranger Raid on St. Francis   67

Francis M. Hoeflinger

U. S. Air Force Medals of Honor   77

Justin Brian McDonald

Students of War: Books and the Education of the
American Continental Army   90

Anne Midgley

A Paratrooper's Foresight: General James Gavin and the Health of the
United States   109

Timothy T. Tutka

Book Reviews   124

From the Editor

Welcome to the ninth issue of the American Public University System (APUS)'s *Saber and Scroll Journal.* We are pleased that the APUS historical community responded so enthusiastically to the spring 2014 issue call for papers. This combined spring-summer 2014 issue contains feature articles and book reviews reflecting the broad range of history interests across our scholarly community.

As most *Saber and Scroll Journal* readers are aware, the journal team has recently undergone some changes. I would like especially to thank two team members, Melanie Thornton and William Potter for their contributions. Melanie has recently completed her Public History master's degree at APUS and retired from her role as a Saber and Scroll editor, after providing us with her expertise and hard work in the creation of several of our past issues. I want to extend a special thanks to William Potter, who stepped in as the interim Editor-In-Chief to allow me to concentrate on my thesis this spring. Additionally, I would like to thank our copy editor, DeAnna Stevens, who not only formats our journal, but who also designs the beautiful artwork that graces its cover. We are pleased to welcome several new members to the team, including Susanne Watts, Aida Dias, and Michael Majerczyk as well as our faculty advisor, Emily Herff.

We continue to seek additional volunteers to help create a superb student-led history journal; if interested, please contact any member of the current journal team.

Please enjoy this issue of the Saber and Scroll Journal!

Anne Midgley
Interim Editor-In-Chief

Henry Clay is Dead: The End of Compromise in Antebellum America

Joseph Cook

As a member of the Congress's Great Triumvirate, which also included Daniel Webster and John C. Calhoun, Henry Clay established a reputation as "The Great Compromiser" for his repeated success at mediating between competing interests and maintaining national union throughout his five troublesome decades of public service. Abraham Lincoln called him the "beau ideal of a statesman,"[1] and this sentiment was shared by many throughout not only the United States, but also abroad in Europe and in Latin America where he was a fervent supporter of independence movements. His final great act on the national stage was the Compromise of 1850, aimed at sorting out the sectional troubles that resulted from the Mexican War – a war that Clay had vigorously opposed. He worked hard to reach that compromise solution, but being aged and in ill health, he was forced to relinquish some of his leadership responsibilities to a younger generation – namely Stephen Douglas. Clay died in 1852, and the following several years only accelerated the nation's course toward disunion and civil war. In historical retrospection, this could spark curiosity concerning the effect that an immortal Henry Clay may have had on the great national emergency. Such speculation may be academically meaningless, but it is useful to examine several issues related to his exit from the national stage: the conditions of the nation at the time of Clay's death, the level of success he found in his final years in terms of orchestrating compromises, the nation's reaction to his death, and the ways in which he was remembered at the time of the secession crisis of 1860.

Henry Clay and Andrew Jackson cast their tremendous shadows over half-a-century of American politics. They were bitter political rivals – the fathers of rival parties, the Whigs and Democrats, respectively – and their personal disdain for each other was palpable. "This great Republic has been convulsed to its centre by the great divisions which have sprung from their respective opinions, policy, and personal destinies," Congressman Charles Faulkner proclaimed.[2] Yet these two titans of the antebellum era were equally committed to the preservation of the American union. The movement toward division of the nation was led by one of the other members of the Great Triumvirate: John C. Calhoun, an erstwhile ally of Clay in the Congress who had heated clashes with the fiery President Jackson. The Nullification Crisis of 1832 prompted the bizarre political spectacle of Andrew Jackson and Henry Clay working together, passing the Force Bill and a new tariff to alleviate the troubles and save the country. In this age of political titans, the preservation of the republic trumped party politics – even among bitter rivals like Clay and Jackson.

An illustrative event of the importance of national preservation occurred during the presidency of Jackson's protégé, James K. Polk, who defeated Clay in the perennial presidential loser's bitterest electoral failure. On February 4, 1848, Clay paid a visit to President Polk in the Executive Mansion. The President "hadn't anticipated a courtesy call from the man who had raged against just about every political initiative of the Jackson-Polk party for two decades."[3] They talked of each other's families, and joked of supporting each other if either ran for the presidency again (producing "a hearty laugh").

> The touching episode reflected an underlying reality of American politics: However intensely the battles are fought and however copiously the animosities flow, all parties are expected to accept the political outcomes in good grace and refrain from the kinds of personal enmities that could undermine the delicate balance of democracy.[4]

For two men who worked for the improvement and prestige of the American nation – divergent as their visions for the country may have been – the era they knew was clearly coming to an end. Mr. Polk's War, which Clay had vigorously opposed, was destined to exacerbate the sectional debates within the nation and bring a new generation of leaders to the forefront. As historian Robert Merry wrote, "These were the two surviving lions of the old politics, and of course senior lions like to mingle with other lions."[5] This was a slightly bizarre statement by Merry, as both Calhoun and Triumvirate-member Daniel Webster were still alive in 1848. However, Merry was correct in writing,

> The old era of politics was fading now, and these gentlemen of the old era were fading with it. Looking back on all the battles and battle scars of their political rivalry, they shared a commonality of nostalgia that could never be appreciated by the younger lions of either party vying for dominance of the nation.[6]

This next generation of lions – men like William Seward, Stephen Douglas, and William Yancey – inherited the partisan animosity of their political predecessors but without the national spirit and willingness to compromise. Seward, the New York leader of free soil Whigs, spoke of an "irrepressible conflict" between North and South, and "admitted to plotting that … slavery zealotry might goad Southern Democrats and thus the Slavepower-dominated Democratic Party to demand outrageously much for slavery. Then Whigs could whip up greater anti-southern – and anti-Democratic Party – hatreds in the North."[7] Yancey became a leader of the fire-eaters, pushing for secession if the Slave Power was ever threatened. Douglas searched for the political middle-ground but ultimately only muddled himself in ambiguity and confusion. Historian David M.

Potter could not resist the urge to compare this cast of characters to a literary or staged drama. Webster was "the kind of senator that Richard Wagner might have created at the height of his powers" and was "Jove-like;" Calhoun was "the most majestic champion of error since Milton's Satan in *Paradise Lost*; and Clay, the old Conciliator, who had already saved the Union twice and now [in 1850] came out of retirement to save it … once again before he died."[8] These three were the "relics of a golden age, who still towered like giants above the creatures of a later time."[9] Among those of the later time, "there was an able supporting cast – Seward, [John] Bell, Douglas, [Thomas Hart] Benton, [Lewis] Cass, [Jefferson] Davis, [Salmon] Chase – who would have been stars on any other stage."[10] The failure of Clay and Webster to sew up the incomplete national fabric – begun by the Founders – left the issue in this next generation's hands, with the disciples of Calhoun's error and their radical adversaries in the North setting the drama on a course toward national tragedy.

Clay personally mistrusted several of these younger men – dubious about their commitment to the integrity of the nation. Some of this was personal; since 1839, he had felt betrayed by William Henry Seward (and fellow New York Whig leader, Thurlow Weed), who Clay believed had abandoned the principles of the party and been personally deceptive after Seward supported Winfield Scott and William Henry Harrison for the presidential nomination over Clay. This came after Clay had received assurances from a friend in New York that "The Governor [Seward] & Thurlow Weed … are not only friendly to your election, but warmly & zealously so – but they deem it inexpedient to make public declarations of their preference."[11] Despite himself being a master of backroom politics – as a legislative leader must be – Clay had a deep mistrust for men such as Seward who professed support privately but publicly did not follow through on the promise. He also feared the effect of the abolitionist movement growing in the Northern states. "Show that the agitation of the [slavery] question in the free States, will first destroy all harmony, and finally lead to disunion," he advised Calvin Colton in 1843. "That the consequences of disunion – perpetual war – the extinction of the African race – ultimate military despotism."[12]

Clay worried about the abolitionist belief – expressed by Seward in the Congress – that "there is a higher law than the Constitution."[13] Considering the influence that Seward wielded in the 1850s, the power he was later perceived as possessing within the Lincoln administration, and his differing methods from those of Henry Clay, an examination of this speech is valuable – as it echoed throughout the 1850s in the paranoid minds of secessionist Southerners. Seward, opposing Clay's final grand act on the national stage – the Compromise of 1850 – proclaimed that, "I am opposed to any such compromise, in any and all forms ... because, while admitting the purity and the patriotism of all from whom it is my misfortune to differ, I think all legislative compromises radically wrong and essentially vicious."[14] To Clay, this statement must have stung as strongly as Seward's perceived betrayal in the Whig convention of 1839. The time of loyal opposition like that Clay embodied during the administration of President Polk was clearly fading into the past. The sections were dividing along a deepening chasm. Webster spoke four days before Mr. Seward, delivering his most famous address, in which he spoke "not as a Massachusetts man, nor as a northern man, but as an American, and a member of the Senate of the United States."[15] Unfortunately, the rest of that speech is largely forgotten by historical memory. Webster, echoing Clay, promoted the power and compromising ability of the Congress, stating, "It is fortunate that there is a Senate of the United States; a body not yet moved from its propriety ... and a body to which the country looks with confidence, for wise, moderate, patriotic, and healing counsels ... in the midst of strong agitations."[16] He lamented, "The imprisoned winds are let loose. The East, the West, the North, and the stormy South, all combine to throw the whole ocean into commotion."[17] Webster attributed more of the storm to the South than to abolitionist agitators in the North, but like his fellow aging titan Clay, he feared for the future of the union due to the growing antagonism toward compromise.

In regard to the "stormy South" and its leaders who threatened secession, Clay was deeply troubled. Like Webster, Clay feared that the younger generation of legislators was losing sight of the national responsibilities of the Congress's duties. "I am not surprised at your mortification by having imputed to you the epithet old politician,"[18] he wrote to Nathan Sargent. "If I had yielded to similar feelings, I should a thousand times have abandoned politics for ever. But we must recollect that it is our *Country* that we have to serve, and that it is our duty to serve it, altho' treated unjustly."[19] This liberal sense of American nationalism was being crushed by the sectional and ethnic concerns of the 1850s, though.

Such fiery elements were already growing in numbers, power, and influence by the time Webster and Clay exited the national stage. To Clay and his Kentucky ally John J. Crittenden, both sides were guilty of driving the nation toward disunion and war. Clay and Crittenden were "quick to deplore abolitionists and Republican free soilers as dangerous to domestic peace ... [and] equally critical of southern fire-eaters."[20] As far as the two aged Kentucky statesmen were concerned, the antagonistic efforts of the two sides ignored the fact that California and the other territories would likely not be settled for decades, and thus were making "a present evil out of an apprehension of a future one never likely to occur."[21] Both proponents of gradual, compensated emancipation, these two Border

State leaders deplored the enthusiasm of the younger generation. Their own vision – which inspired the young Whig Abraham Lincoln – had "'the three main features – gradual – compensation – and the vote of the people,' all of which abolitionists abhorred."[22] Lincoln, the Clay disciple, referred to abolitionists as "fiends," and stated, "I can express all my views on the slavery question by quotations from Henry Clay."[23] To those who ultimately formed the conservative wing of the Republican Party, after the collapse of the Whigs, Henry Clay continued to be an idol in his unionist and gradualist ideologies. Accordingly, Lincoln once proclaimed, "If ... there be any man in the republican party who is impatient of ... the constitutional obligations bound around it, he is misplaced, and ought to find a place somewhere else."[24] Extremes were the enemy to Clay and his ilk, because they closed the minds of men to the value of compromise for the sake of the nation.

The Compromise of 1850 demonstrated the decreased effectiveness of compromise on the national stage over the slavery question, and also made clear the growing resistance to it as a legislative method. Clay was unable to push it through himself, even with his silvery tongue and rejuvenated personal charm. He was forced to turn to a member of that younger generation he mistrusted, Stephen Douglas of Illinois, to finally push the compromise through by individual measures – with purely sectional lines of support. Another Westerner, the Little Giant Douglas could logically have been seen as a fine potential replacement for the old giant. Yet Douglas's measures failed to assuage sectional furor from the very start – beginning with Clay's proposals in 1850 and culminating with the disastrous Kansas -Nebraska Act in 1854.

The Compromise of 1850 created no lasting sense of national relief. Its most controversial measure was the new Fugitive Slave Law. A concession to the Slave Power of the South, the law put the onus of maintaining slavery in the face of runaways on the Northern population. This accelerated and bolstered the agitation of the abolitionists, and actively engaged non-abolitionist Northerners in the moral debate over slavery for the first time in a direct manner. Ulysses S. Grant recalled the effect of this in his memoirs. "This was a degradation which the North would not permit any longer than until they could get the power to expunge such laws from the statute books," he wrote.[25] "Prior to the time of these encroachments the great majority of the people of the North had no particular quarrel with slavery, so long as they were not forced to have it themselves. But they were not willing to play the role of police for the South in the protection of this particular institution."[26]

Clay seemed to believe that the Northern public would perform their civic duty in his broad sense of nationalism, recognizing the threat to the republic and the union, but the Fugitive Slave Act did as much to drive a wedge between the sections as any issue. It confirmed the wickedness of Henry Clay in the minds of abolitionists, who had railed against Clay for decades as one of the leaders of the American Colonization Society (hereafter, ACS). William Lloyd Garrison's *The Liberator* waged a decades-long campaign against the ACS, celebrating that "Ten times the number of slaves colonize themselves in Canada every year, at a much less expense than is incurred by the Colonization Society."[27] In opposition to the Fugitive Slave Act, *The Liberator* condemned the "tyranny of a heartless and God-defying government," and urged the protection, employment, and provision for the fugitive slave population.[28] The epitome of that heartless government was the contemptible compromiser, Henry Clay. The *Liberator* ultimately did not waste much ink on eulogizing the man who held the union together by surrendering elements of their philosophy to the South. However, other abolitionist newspapers, notably Horace Greeley's *New York Daily Tribune*, painted adoring portraits of the great departed statesman. "Mr. Clay was an aspirant, but a noble one," the paper stated, in the midst of a full page of coverage. Perhaps forgotten by other abolitionists, the *Tribune* paid tribute to Clay's efforts as a young Kentucky legislator to insert gradual emancipation into his state's constitution, "a suggestion which was over-ruled by their short-sighted egotism" and by "slaveholding selfishness."[29]

When Clay passed from the world at the end of June in 1852, the news was shockingly placed secondary in many papers due to the near-simultaneous nominations of Franklin Pierce and Winfield Scott for the presidency. Pierce's administration eventually was marked by the utter failure of Douglas's efforts to fill the shoes of the Great Compromiser, stumbling for political middle ground by taking the question out of Congress's hands and placing it entirely in the hands of the people. But the Whigs' nomination of Winfield Scott at the same moment that their aged standard-bearer was departing the world led many to assess the future of the party. The *National Era* of Washington, DC expressed hope for the abolitionist cause: "While a superficial observer would see … in the multitudinous assemblages who hurrah for Pierce or Scott… the ruin of the Anti-Slavery cause, those who look deeper into things perceive a deeper, powerful, and gigantic sentiment against slavery pervading the country."[30] Again the *Tribune* was a strong exception to this trend, committing only a short paragraph to announce, "Gen. Scott's Letter accepting the Whig nomination for President will be found in our columns … As any allusion to the points that we specially approve therein would probably excite hostility on the part of others, we will simply say that, as a whole, we *like* it."[31] Then, in a sarcastic shot at Clay and any others who criticized the activism of the abolitionist press, the short paragraph concluded, "There can't be any treason in *that*."[32]

Others saw no subtlety in the nomination of Scott, who was well-known to be supported by Seward – which would very likely have met the disapproval of Clay due to Seward's opposition to national compromise. One element of Scott's letter of acceptance would have satisfied Mr. Clay:

> Convinced that harmony or good will between the different quarters of our broad country is essential to the present and future interests of the Republic, and with a devotion to those interests that can know no South and no North, I should neither countenance nor tolerate any sedition, disorder, faction, or re-sistance to the laws, or to the Union.[33]

The Democratic *Brooklyn Daily Eagle* reported on Clay's death, stating, "Every heart seems to feel that a great man has gone from among us."[34] But on the same page, it also traced the deceitfulness of William Henry Seward, and mocked Scott's acceptance letter as "another 'hasty plate of soup' production."[35] The *Covington Journal* of Kentucky, meanwhile, expressed the belief that "Mr. Seward, it seems, wouldn't accept a cabinet appointment from President Scott, and most certainly he couldn't get it if he would."[36]

There was great anxiety among the Democratic press and the moderate Whig press concerning the influence Seward would hold in a Scott presidency – something that would have alarmed Clay. The *Fayetteville Observer*, a Democratic newspaper in Tennessee, fore-told that the nomination of General Scott, supported by Seward, would serve to "denationalize the Whig party, and to select a sec-tional [nominee]."[37] It then warned its readers, "Mr. Seward, when Gen. Scott is nominated, will be inaugurated, emphatically, into the position of ruler and controller of the Whig party of the nation."[38] Hitting a theme that would echo in the South among fire-eaters, it reminded all, "The Wm. H. Seward spoken of … is the veritable, the identical originator and propagator of the 'higher law doctrine' which is so justly condemned and despised by every lover of the country."[39] The deceased Clay could have been counted among those lovers of the country. Connecting the issue of Seward's influence to the late statesman, the paper then explained, "As soon as the compromise measures passed, all the papers under Mr. Seward's control raised up the name of Gen. Scott ... as their candidate for the presidency," set upon "abolitionizing of the Whig party" by elevating Seward as Scott's unspoken puppet-master.[40]

Clay's Whig Party was indeed doomed to division and collapse. Many Whig papers and eulogizers, though, ignored the troubled state and uncertain future of the party and produced flowery tributes to their fallen leader whose policies were soon to be discarded as the party shifted and ultimately evaporated. The *New York Times* published a number of these tributes, ranging from the report of an "English Judgment of Henry Clay" – which proclaimed him "among the first class of American worthies ... to be regretted by the world" – to the various eulogies coming from all over the country, including by Clay's former vice-presidential candidate, Theodore Frelinghuysen of New Jersey.[41] According to the *Times*, "The heavy blow, long suspended, has fallen at last. Henry Clay, the renowned and the peerless, has gone to his rest."[42] In its full-page tribute, the *Times* reported that Clay was simply "too great to be President."[43] Clay's death was mourned by all throughout the nation – with the exception of some radical abolitionists and extreme southern fire-eaters – "From every quarter of the Union, from all parties and from all classes."[44] One of the most intriguing pieces of coverage the *Times* provided concerning Clay's death was its printing of Seward's remarks on the Senate floor on the matter. He obliquely criticized Clay in the undertones of his florid praise, mentioning that "History will confirm ... that Conservatism was the interest of the nation and the responsibility of its Rulers, during the period in which he flourished."[45] Unspoken in this was Seward's belief that Clay's conservatism and compromising were things of the past. He proceeded to encourage others who knew Clay longer to speak in his place. Finally, he declined to discuss Clay's legislative achievements at any length, but instead mentioned his belief, "His personal qualities may be discussed without apprehension."[46] William Henry Seward was leading the Whig Party in a new direction, and he was not going to use up his time on the floor praising the old methods and the old giant.

Some Whigs would not let the legacy of Clay die, even while the party changed and collapsed. Frelinghuysen elaborated on all the areas of life in which Henry Clay was a great man, and then turned to his reputation: "It has been sometimes said, that Mr. Clay was not popular. This must depend upon the interpretation of the term. There is a popularity, which, like the gourd, comes up in a night, and departs in a night, and no man can tell us what has become of it … Mr. C. had none of this."[47] Turning to what Clay *did* have, he continued, "And there is a popularity … [that] grows on, the more healthfully, because of trials … This popularity has another element. It lives beyond the grave — the sepulcher cannot impair the securities of a good name."[48] According to the New Jersey Whig, Clay would be dearly missed by the nation in any time of trouble.[49] Out west, an idolizer of Clay delivered Illinois's official eulogy for the fallen Whig leader. Unabashedly, Abraham Lincoln extolled Clay's personal traits and his professional accomplishments and efforts. "Alas! Who can realize that Henry Clay is dead! Who can realize that never again that majestic form shall rise in the council-chambers of his country to beat back the storms of anarchy which may threaten!"[50] Reflecting Clay's sense of liberal nationalism, Lincoln continued, "Henry Clay belonged to his country — to the world, mere party cannot claim men like him. His career has been national — his fame has filled the earth – his memory will endure to 'the last syllable of recorded time.' Henry Clay is dead!"[51]

When the great national chasm came, with South Carolina seceding from the Union in December of 1860, it was natural to turn thoughts back to the compromising efforts of Henry Clay. His former Kentucky colleague, John Crittenden, failed in the role of compromiser during the secession crisis. Lincoln was president, still keeping the words and example of Henry Clay in his mind. William Seward, who had opposed Clay's methods, ironically stood at Lincoln's right hand. The Central Campaign Club of New York held a reception that drew attention due to the fact, "It is remarkable that there should have been but two receptions, until tonight, in this room. One was to Daniel Webster, the other to Henry Clay, and a third is now to Abraham Lincoln."[52] Meanwhile, Seward toured the North, where

> Some compared it with receptions the Whigs used to give Henry Clay in his tours through the Northern States. There is one difference to be remembered in considering the significance of these ovations to the great statesman. There was no striking contrast in Mr. Clay's case. It was never unpopular to honor him.[53]

Mr. Seward personally would have likely disagreed with this *New York Times* report, which continued, "It was never unpopular and almost a disgrace to be a 'Clay man.' But how recent the time when to be a 'Seward man' required the highest moral courage."[54] For decades, one of these two great statesmen guided the Whig party toward compromise as a loose national organization; yet the second man had used the most recent decade to bolt from the Whigs for a new party, after helping to damage the national nature of the old structure.

Most importantly, the new Republican leaders – Lincoln and Seward – former Whigs with drastically different opinions of Henry Clay, could take inspiration for the coming struggle from Clay's unionism. Seward's early commitment to forcing the seceded states was lukewarm at best, but Lincoln was resolute. Writing of secession in the 1840s, Clay had proclaimed, "For my own part, I utterly deny the existence of any such right, and I think an attempt to exercise it ought to be resisted to the last extremity; for it is in fact a question of Union or no Union."[55] The *New York Times* proclaimed that Clay would personally be "for lopping off the hydra head of secession by the strong arm of the offended law." His stance was recounted as such:

> There can be but one possible answer. The power, the authority, and the dignity of the Government ought to be maintained, and resistance put down at every hazard ... My belief is that if it should be applied to South Carolina, in the event of her secession, she would be speedily reduced to obedience, and that the Union, instead of being weakened, would acquire additional strength.[57]

This was Lincoln's position in the secession crisis – that swift and stern action against the seceded states would restore the union, and that all efforts should be exhausted for that cause. Taking inspiration from Clay's speeches concerning the Compromise of 1850, Lincoln's inaugural address alluded to the national "mystic chords of memory" and "the better angels of our nature."[58] Critically important in the strategy of preserving the integrity of the nation, "Kentucky, which holds the ashes of Henry Clay, stands by the Union!"[59] Henry Clay was dead, but as Frelinghuysen and Lincoln had predicted in their eulogies, his guidance was missed and his shadow was felt in the great national disaster.

Notes

[1] David S. Heidler and Jeanne T. Heidler, *Henry Clay: the Essential American* (New York: Random House, 2010), 431.

[2] Heidler and Heidler, xiii.

[3] Robert W. Merry, *A Country of Vast Designs: James K. Polk, the Mexican War and the Conquest of the American Continent* (New York: Simon and Schuster, 2009), 419.

[4] Merry, 419.

[5] Ibid., 419.

[6] Ibid., 419-420.

[7] Bruce Levine, *Half Slave and Half Free: the Roots of the Civil War* (New York: Hill and Wang, 1992), 15; William W. Freehling, *The Road to Disunion: Secessionists at Bay, 1776-1854* (New York: Oxford University Press, 1990), 555. When the secession crisis broke out, Seward devised bizarre compromise solutions including calls for a war against some foreign power to unite the sections, but his record throughout the 1850s was one of abject rejection of compromise. Seward's efforts to reunite the nation are detailed in Walter Stahr, *Seward: Lincoln's Indispensable Man* (New York: Simon and Schuster, 2012).

[8] David M. Potter, *The Impending Crisis, 1848-1861* (New York: Harper, 1976), 98.

[9] Ibid.

[10] Ibid.

[11] Robert Seager, ed., *The Whig Leader, January 1, 1837-December 31, 1843*, vol. 9 of *The Papers of Henry Clay* (Lexington: University Press of Kentucky, 1988), 287.

[12] Seager, ed., *The Whig Leader*, 852.

[13] *Congressional Globe*, 31st Cong., 1st sess., 1850, 260-269. Located within the Appendix of the 31st Congress, 1st Session.

[14] *Congressional Globe*, 31st Cong., 1st sess.

[15] Ibid.

[16] Ibid.

[17] *Congressional Globe*, 31st Cong., 1st Sess. 269. Located within the Appendix of the 31st Congress, 1st Session. Any thoughts of the Congress being a place "not yet moved from its propriety" or where the country could look "with confidence, for wise, moderate, patriotic, and healing counsels," was shattered in the 1850s when Southern Congressman Preston Brooks physically assaulted and almost killed abolitionist Senator Charles Sumner.

[18] Seager, ed., *The Whig Leader*, 853. Sargent was a Whig who served as Sergeant-at-Arms of the House of Representatives during the 1840s.

[19] Seager, ed., *The Whig Leader*, 853.

[20] Douglas R. Egerton, *Year of Meteors: Stephen Douglas, Abraham Lincoln, and the Election that Brought on the Civil War* (New York: Bloomsbury Press, 2010), 85.

[21] Egerton, 85.

[22] Allen C. Guelzo, "Lincoln and the Abolitionists," *Wilson Quarterly* 24, no. 4 (Autumn 2000), 63.

[23] Guelzo, 65.

[24] Ibid.

[25] Ulysses S. Grant, *Personal Memoirs* (New York: Penguin, 1999), 634.

[26] Grant, 634.

[27] "Colonization Society," *The Liberator*, March 31, 1843.

[28] "To the Friends of the Fugitive," *The Liberator*, November 8, 1850.

[29] "Death of Henry Clay," *New York Daily Tribune*, June 30, 1852, p. 4.

[30] "Letter from New York," *The National Era*, July 1, 1852.

[31] *New York Daily Tribune*, June 30, 1852, p. 5 c.1.

[32] Ibid.

[33] "Gen. Scott's Letter of Acceptance," *Brooklyn Daily Eagle*, June 30, 1852, p. 2, c. 3.

[34] "Mr. Clay's Last Moments," *Brooklyn Daily Eagle*, June 30, 1852, p. 2, c. 4. The first two columns were dedicated to advocating for Franklin Pierce's candidacy.

[35] Gen. Scott's Letter of Acceptance," *Brooklyn Daily Eagle*, June 30, 1852, p. 2, c. 3.

[36] "Letter from Mr. Seward," *Covington Journal*, July 10, 1852.

[37] "To the Whigs of Lincoln County," *Fayetteville Observer*, July 1, 1852, p. 2, c. 1-4.

[38] Ibid.

[39] Ibid.

[40] "To the Whigs of Lincoln County," *Fayetteville Observer*, July 1, 1852, p. 2, c. 1-4. The same charge of Seward pulling the strings was later made during the presidency of Abraham Lincoln.

[41] "English Judgment of Henry Clay," *New York Times*, July 26, 1852.

[42] "Death of Henry Clay: Sketch of His Life and Public Career," *New York Times*, June 30, 1852.

[43] Ibid.

[44] "The Death of Henry Clay," *New York Times*, July 1, 1852; "Henry Clay: Eulogy Delivered by Hon. Theodore Frelinghuysen, at Newark, on the 13th of July," *New York Times*, July 15, 1852.

[45] "Henry Clay – Living and Dead: Mr. Seward's Remarks," *New York Times*, July 2, 1852.

[46] Ibid.

[47] "Henry Clay: Eulogy Delivered by Hon. Theodore Frelinghuysen, at Newark, on the 13th of July," *New York Times*, July 15, 1852.

[48] Ibid.

[49] Ibid.

[50] Abraham Lincoln, "Eulogy on Henry Clay," Abraham Lincoln Online, http://www.abrahamlincolnonline.org/lincoln/speeches/clay.htm (accessed November 7, 2013).

[51] Abraham Lincoln, "Eulogy on Henry Clay," Abraham Lincoln Online, http://www.abrahamlincolnonline.org/lincoln/speeches/clay.htm (accessed November 7, 2013). For deep meanings of Lincoln's eulogy for Clay, see Mark E. Neely, "American Nationalism in the Image of Henry Clay: Abraham Lincoln's Eulogy on Henry Clay in Context." *The Registry of the Kentucky Historical Society* 106, no. 3/4 (Summer/Autumn 2008): 537-570.

[52] "Mr. Lincoln's Address to the Republican Committees," *New York Times*, February 20, 1861.

53 "Gov. Seward's Tour," *New York Times*, Sept. 4, 1860.

54 Ibid.

55 "What Henry Clay Thought of Secession," *New York Times*, December 26, 1860.

56 "What Shall Be Done with a Seceding State? Henry Clay's Opinion," *New York Times*, November 15, 1860.

57 "What Shall Be Done with a Seceding State? Henry Clay's Opinion," *New York Times*, November 15, 1860.

58 Egerton, *Year of Meteors*, 321-322.

59 "Light from Kentucky!" *New York Times*, January 26, 1861. The first two columns were dedicated to advocating for Franklin Pierce's candidacy.

Bibliography

Bordewich, Fergus M. *America's Great Debate: Henry Clay, Stephen A. Douglas, and the Compromise that Preserved the Union*. New York: Simon and Schuster, 2012.

Egerton, Douglas R. *Year of Meteors: Stephen Douglas, Abraham Lincoln, and the Election that Brought on the Civil War*. New York: Bloomsbury Press, 2010.

Freehling, William W. *The Road to Disunion: Secessionists at Bay, 1776-1854*. New York: Oxford University Press, 1990.

Grant, Ulysses S. *Personal Memoirs*. New York: Penguin, 1999.

Guelzo, Allen C. "Lincoln and the Abolitionists." *Wilson Quarterly* 24, no. 4 (Autumn 2000): 58-70.

Hay, John and John G. Nicolay. *Abraham Lincoln: a History*. 10 vols. New York: the Century Company, 1890.

Heidler, David S., and Jeanne T. Heidler. *Henry Clay: the Essential American*. New York: Random House, 2010.

Holt, Michael F. *The Political Crisis of the 1850s*. New York: Wiley, 1978.

Levine, Bruce. *Half Slave and Half Free: the Roots of the Civil War*. New York: Hill and Wang, 1992.

Lincoln, Abraham. "Eulogy on Henry Clay." Abraham Lincoln Online. http://www.abrahamlincolnonline.org/lincoln/speeches/clay.htm (accessed November 7, 2013).

Merry, Robert W. *A Country of Vast Designs: James K. Polk, the Mexican War and the Conquest of the American Continent*. New York: Simon and Schuster, 2009.

Neely, Mark E. "American Nationalism in the Image of Henry Clay: Abraham Lincoln's Eulogy on Henry Clay in Context." *The Registry of the Kentucky Histor-*

ical Society 106, no. 3/4 (Summer/Autumn 2008): 537-570.

Potter, David M. *The Impending Crisis, 1848-1861*. New York: Harper, 1976.

Schurz, Carl. *Henry Clay*. New York: Houghton, Mifflin, and Company, 1899.

Seager, Robert. "Henry Clay and the Politics of Compromise and Non-Compromise." *The Register of the Kentucky Historical Society* 85, no. 1 (Winter 1987): 1-28.

-----, ed. *The Whig Leader, January 1, 1837-December 31, 1843*. Vol. 9 of *The Papers of Henry Clay*. Lexington: University Press of Kentucky, 1988.

Simpson, Craig. "Political Compromise and the Protection of Slavery." *The Virginia Magazine of History and Biography* 83, no. 4 (October 1975): 387-405.

Stahr, Walter. *Seward: Lincoln's Indispensable Man*. New York: Simon and Schuster, 2012.

U.S. Congress. *Congressional Globe*. 31st Cong., 1st sess., 1850.

Τύχη: Fortune, Fate and Chance in Herodotus and Thucydides
Benjamin Sorensen

Man has always wished to be able to explain incomprehensible phenomena and has turned to supernatural entities to elucidate the workings of the world. Divination, such as looking at the entrails of sacrificed animals or scrying into crystal balls to help understand these phenomena, has been long employed by people. Using oracles, such as those employed at Delphi or even the more modern use of Tarot, has been employed to see if the gods favored man's laudable or despicable endeavors. Many natural phenomena were so powerful that certain gods were attributed to these powers, and emotions that often misguided people's activities were also given divine entities which not only ruled these emotions but also explained the vagaries caused by them. These gods were jealous, frivolous, and yet so powerful that they could "bring the lofty low."[1]

However, there were often situations that were outside the realms of certain gods that could not be explained by natural phenomena or by the wills or power of men. These most inexplicable of occurrences, these moments that seemingly arbitrarily decided the fortunes of man, were given to the goddess Tyche (Τύχη). She, according to Hesiod, was the offspring of the Ocean and Tethys,[2] and according to Pindar, a daughter of Zeus the Deliverer.[3] Her ability to change the course of history and the fate of man was often cited, and these changes were seemingly on a whim. She lives on today when a person speaks of a change in "fortune" (from the Latin *Fortuna*,) for better or worse, as well as in the sociological theory of indeterminism of Charles Pierce (which he called *tychism*).[4]

The word "τύχη" as "fortune" rather than a cognomen for a pure deity also found its way into common usage in Ancient Greece and is used extensively in the works of Herodotus and Thucydides. Though at first glance this does not seem to signify a departure from the spirituality of Ancient Greek civilization, the fact that both are more than ready to prove that man's misfortune or good fortune is his own doing denotes a rationalist world-view that other great writers, and even later Greek and Roman historians, do not share and possibly cannot readily comprehend. This absence of Τύχη is not just a novelty brought on by Greek reliance on empiricism; in fact it is an amazing analytical change in cognizance and understanding especially in light of the phenomena that were readily attributed to the Gods in Classical Greece. Even Polybius, the Greek historian of the rise of Rome, writing at a later date still quips that "Fortune has guided almost all the affairs of the world in one direction and has forced them to incline towards one and the same end."[5] This statement shows the very human need to find a reason for even the inexplicable; it lends logic to an otherwise entropic existence.

It is not that people became more superstitious as time went on, as we have the entire *Theogony* from Hesiod as well as the epics *The Iliad* and *The Odyssey* by Homer to show us the esteem given to both gods and heroes by the Ancient Greeks of their time. For later religious devotion, one only has to look at the complaints raised against Pericles during the Athenian plague to see the fervency of the religious citizens in Thucydides' times. Therefore, the general acceptance of religion remained for the most part unchanged in Greece even though sophists and philosophers began to express doubt. Pericles and his favorite, Protagoras were often cited as being irreverent to the gods, and these claims would not have been made if the general population did not hold beliefs in religious traditions.

Each god, given attributes that come from the vagaries of natural phenomena, was also a protector of certain aspects of life. Athena, for example, was the patroness of Athens and the goddess of the hunt. Zeus, the most powerful of the gods, used a lightning bolt as his weapon of choice. Poseidon ruled over the ocean and earthquakes. Aphrodite was the goddess of love and sexuality, born when Cronos lopped off Ouranos' genitals with a sickle and threw them into the sea.[6]

However, Tyche (Τύχη) was a goddess that was given jurisdiction over the destinies and fates of men and nations. She was often represented as a most fickle entity, born of Tethys and Okeanos according to the *Theogony*.[7] Her whims would either lift a man to fame or destroy the family and nation of a king. She was, in fact, a ready-made scapegoat for the inexplicable events of history; she could be the explanation for unexpected wealth or the decimation of a people by plague. Though these could also be attributed to the Μοίραι (known as the Fates in English), they were mainly attributed to Tyche as a titular deity. She was the goddess that controlled the factors that could exalt men and level nations. She was "less powerful than fate,"[8] but still a singular force in man's destiny. The fact that she was represented with a cornucopia signifies that her whims were always to the benefit of man.[9]

However, her treatment in Herodotus' *The Histories* and Thucydides' *The Peloponnesian Wars* is amazing in not what is attributed to her but often by what is not attributed to her whims. Though these two historians were active when the Sophists and the philosophers were coming of age and when human reason was to become the basis of understanding, one must remember that the Greeks still had a theology to explain the inexplicable. Plato was trying to define the "good," but Athens still paid heed to oracles and lauded Athena as the patron goddess. Socrates was executed for "neglect of the gods whom the city worships" as well as for "corrupting the young."[10] Therefore, this dichotomy of the Greeks' understanding of natural phenomena as well as causality must be remembered to fully appreciate the amazing advances of both Herodotus and Thucydides. They could have attributed every inexplicable act to the divine, more so to Tyche, but instead they both chose to attribute man's fate to his own character flaws and subsequent actions. God (Θεον) occasionally makes an appearance, as in Herodotus' line "Many things make it plain to me that the hand of God is active in human affairs..."[11] but this is to describe coincidences that "prove" divine intervention, much akin to divination of animal entrails or deciphering nebulous oracles. He readily cites the timing of certain events to account for God's presence, and it is in retrospect that divine intervention becomes apparent. Herodotus assigns the hand of God to only those coincidences that prove by the order of their inherent forms, and not by the anarchy of the situations, that the supernatural is at work. Tyche, however, would have been more chaotic in deciding the fate of men, armies, and nations.

However, looking at fate (τύχη with a small tau) in Herodotus' works is enlightening in its seeming humanism. When he first discusses the origins of the Greeks, he tells us that "nearly all the gods came to Greece from Egypt."[12] He then expands this to say:

> But it was only—if I may so put it—the day before yesterday that the Greeks came to know the origin and form of the various gods, and whether or not all of them had always existed; for Homer and Hesiod are the poets who composed theogonies and described the gods for the Greeks, giving them all their appropriate titles, offices and powers, and they lived, as I believe, not more than four hundred years ago.[13]

He also tells us that the word for god, θεοι, comes from the Greek word for disposers, as they "dispose" laws and order upon mankind.[14] Therefore, with this devout mindset, to *not* attribute whims and vagaries of history on Tyche shows a very large step being taken in an empirical understanding of causality in the human experience. He possibly demonstrates the beginnings of a belief-system like Protagoras': "Concerning the gods I am unable to discover whether they exist or not, or what they are like in form; for there are many hindrances to knowledge, the obscurity of the subject and the brevity of human life. . . Man is the measure of all things."[15] Herodotus certainly believes that the gods have their place in dictating the vagaries of man and he is ready to show their favors towards certain endeavors in his history, but they are no longer the dictators of man's fate. As historiographer and historian, Ernst Breisach points out, "Essentially, Herodotus' list of reasons for the war is a list of human motives."[16] This is very different from Polybius' understanding of Tyche; this later historian believed that the Persian Wars were one instance where the horrors of Tyche were suspended.[17] It is the absence of the divine in the affairs of men that makes Herodotus' work so special; he too could have found grounds for Tyche arresting her wrath or spreading good fortune, but he refrains.

The great classicist H. D. F. Kitto describes this by explaining all Greeks' reliance on reason: "The Greek never doubted for a moment that the universe is not capricious; it obeys Law and is therefore capable of explanation. . . Greek tragedy is built on the faith that in human affairs it is Law that reigns, not chance."[18] However, one would have to ask why then Tyche was even a concept for a goddess if not to function as an explanation of the inexplicable. In fact, historian William Smith in *The Dictionary of Greek and Roman Antiquities* points out that Tyche was given three tools to symbolize her power: the rudder to direct the lives and fates of man, a ball to demonstrate the whimsical nature and unsteadiness of fate, and the cornucopia to symbolize the possible fruits and benefits that she could bestow on man.[19] Further, one only needs to look at the poetry of Pindar to realize that she was often prayed to, as he says in an ode that "she giveth of this and of that."[20]

For Herodotus, however, many of the characters in his histories are prone to speak of "τύχη" as luck. When Croesus and Solon speak of happiness and the happiest man, Solon proves that many have been "unlucky" while rich and those with modest means have been much happier.[21] Here, the fortune that he speaks of is not divine, and neither is the next mention of τύχη divine. Instead, when it comes to light that Harpagos failed to kill Astyages' daughter's son who will become Cyrus, Astyages mentions that this is a pleasant change in "fortune."[22] Again, Herodotus cunningly avoids suggesting that Tyche herself had a hand in this coincidence that the boy survived. In explaining exactly how the boy survived, by Harpagos giving him to a herdsman who kept Cyrus but put his own stillborn child in the elements instead, he negates Tyche of having any part in Cyrus' fulfilling Astyages' dream. He attributes it all to the vagaries of man's actions, however odd the chance that Harpagos should give the child over to a herdsman whose wife had just borne a stillborn child, and the chance that they would think up such a clever method of unintentional deception, actually would be. He assigns the fact that his surrogate mother's name was Κύνω (meaning "bitch") as the impetus for the mythological story of Cyrus' being suckled by hounds to again prove man's ability to decide his own fate, though again any other Greek may have seen that as Tyche's helping Cyrus again to achieve political power.[23] However, this reasoning sufficed for Herodotus; he demonstrated that this would be much more plausible than Tyche's putting the child in the custody of a dog to rear.

But the use of "fortune" here again is also ironic: Astyages speaks of a "change of fortune" in his son's being alive,[24] but then kills Harpagos' son to use as the main course of the celebratory feast—hence changing Harpagos' "fortune" for the worse, and consequently and unwittingly changing also his own for the worse as well.

Again, though, Herodotus would allow fate to play a role in the words of his characters: "Son of Cambyses, over thee the gods keep guard, for otherwise thou wouldst never have come to so much good fortune. Do thou therefore take vengeance on Astyages who is thy murderer, for so far as his will is concerned thou art dead, but by the care of the gods and of me thou art still alive..."[25] Thus are the words in a letter to Cyrus from Harpagos encouraging him to revolt against the king, Astyages. How the letter arrives to Cyrus Herodotus attributes to Harpagos' cunning (its being stuffed in a rabbit and transported by a servant dressed as a hunter), and though the letter itself seems to attribute the previous story of Cyrus' survival to fate or Tyche, we have already seen how Herodotus dispatched with that notion in his narrative. Cyrus' uprising and his inherent strength of personality are almost implied to be the products of good breeding rather than gifts bestowed upon him by the gods, again a moment of Herodotus' ascribing outcomes to man's decisions; even the manner in which he was discovered by Astyages is almost by modern standards "chance."[26] The fact that he acted "kingly" when playing with friends is hardly proof that Cyrus is the king's son by modern standards, but Greeks often put "truth" to different tests than we would undertake today. As philologist Derek Collins points out in his discussion on Greek magic, "Similarly, causal explanation is not universal: what is an incidental cause for one culture might be an efficient one in another."[27] This, when dealing with Herodotus and his understanding of Tyche or chance, must be remembered and expanded: often the difference between the incidental and efficient cause is not cultural but individual.

It takes Herodotus six books to find another situation where τύχη fits again, and in book seven Xerxes the Persian king is getting advice from Artabanos about his planned invasion of Greece. Once again, Tyche is not a goddess defining the outcome of a situation, but rather a concept used in a discussion. Hence, "ἔσσωται δὲ ὑπὸ τῆς τύχης τὸ βούλευμα· ὁ δὲ βουλευσάμενος αἰσχρῶς, εἴ οἱ ἡ τύχη ἐπίσποιτο, εὕρημα εὕρηκε, ἧσσον δὲ οὐδέν οἱ κακῶς βεβούλευται," is translated by the classicist G. C. Macaulay as "the counsel which has been taken is no less good, though it has been defeated by fortune; while he who took counsel badly at first, if good fortune should go with him has lighted on a prize by chance, but none the less for that his counsel was bad."[28] Here, the Persians, and not the Greeks, are contemplating the dangers of Tyche's whims, a situation that lends itself to Herodotus' overall irony. The reader knows that Xerxes is going to lose and the later victories are all attributed to the Greeks' intelligence and vigilance, even though Herodotus sees some form of divine favor to the Greek endeavors.[29] Nonetheless, the good council is apparent to the reader, even though it seems to be Xerxes' divine folly that he does not heed it. Fate, here, is a literary tool; she has not dictated a success or a failure in this case.

One moment where Tyche is attributed, though she is presented in the Greek more as "luck" than as a divine goddess, is in the case of Artemisia's strife during the naval assault.[30] As Artemisia is being pursued by an Athenian ship, she sinks a Calyndian ship. This, perhaps having been an accident, nonetheless ends her danger as the Athenian believes her to be fighting for Greece. Xerxes and his advisors, seeing her maneuver, believe that she sank an Athenian ship in spite of being under duress. This not only saves her during the battle, but puts her into Xerxes' favor. This would have to be so random that only Tyche would have a hand in it; Herodotus is not explicit in this attribution, but his talk of "luck" in this case (he uses the lower-case "τύχη" here) certainly betrays her presence in his opinion.

This is in fact the last instance where Tyche is even implied in Herodotus' history. Again, this is rather surprising considering his willingness to see divine inspiration in the works of man. As the renowned scholar and historian J. B. Bury points out, Herodotus "did not draw a hard and fast line between the human and the divine."[31] However, he was skeptical, and Bury again points out that this was more from the influence of Hecataeus' work than "to the canons of Ionian science or the influence of Ionian philosophy."[32] Herodotus, being devout in his belief in the gods, still found them to be more *laissez-faire* in their treatment of mankind than many of his contemporaries did. As Bury again elucidates, Herodotus shows us many instances of this type of skepticism, and these are more Ionian subtleties than Sophist influences, though they would have culminated in Sophistry.[33] He is also, as Bury says and as is shown by his writings on Artemisia's naval prowess, "an expert in the art of not committing himself."[34] However, as the Byzantinist J. A. S. Evans points out in his work *Herodotus,* Herodotus' relaying of Xerxes dream assigns Xerxes to ". . . tragic destiny; he could not control his fate."[35] This in and of itself shows a determinism that would exclude the influence of Tyche.

Thucydides, on the other hand, was more apt to completely disregard all of the influences of the gods. But he would recognize Tyche as the only external influence on the undertakings of man. However, he believed that Tyche's influence was not defining; ". . . power might have survived and defied its outrages, had it not been for human mismanagement."[36] He would, however, allow citing ". . . severe earthquakes, droughts causing famines, the plague, and eclipses of the sun as its [the Peloponnesian War] portents."[37] He even acknowledges that the most powerful characters in his history will believe in oracles, gods, and omens, but he, himself, does not show personal approval of this.[38] As Breisach says, "Of gods, Thucydides felt, he need not speak."[39]

However, Thucydides' characters found a need to speak of the gods, and even the wise Spartan Archidamus, in his long speech in *The History of the Peloponnesian War,* cites that chance will play a role in the coming war, but the deciding factor will be who best deals with the incalculable, unforeseen situations.[40] To undermine the "freaks of chance" (which imply Tyche's presence), the winner of the war will have to be educated in "the severest school."[41] Tyche will create obstacles in each participant's endeavors throughout the war, but in the end, man will determine his own fate by how he reacts to her whims.

On the other hand, Pericles, the Athenian, shows his Ionian subtlety when speaking again of Tyche. "For sometimes, the course of things is as arbitrary as the plans of man; indeed this is why we usually blame chance for whatever does not happen as we expected," he states.[42] In the original Greek, however, this chance again appears as "τύχη." One can feel Pericles' reference to her caprice as more pronounced as the reader knows what Pericles himself does not: the plague will soon strike him dead, and the war that he is advocating will become the downfall of Athens. As he proclaims to the Athenians only a few paragraphs later, this will be a war of man's ability rather than the whims of Tyche; after all, "did not our fathers resist the Medes. . . more by wisdom than by fortune, more by daring than by strength, did not they beat off the barbarian and advance their affairs to their present height?"[43] He proves that Tyche has always wished to supplant man's enterprises, but the Athenians were always able to outsmart her. He wishes to remind the current generation that they should act no differently.

Archidamus reiterates that Tyche will be present in this war and that "the course of the war cannot be foreseen (Διοτι η τύχη τον πολέμον ειναι αδηλος)."[44] He again, though implies that man is not to falter to Tyche's will, but rather he must rally against it and make the best of each situation to win the war. Events, according to Archidamus and subsequently Thucydides, are often decided by chance, but outcomes are not.

In the debate between Diodotus and Cleon over the fate of the Mitylenians, Thucydides finds a chance to propound his feelings about Tyche herself. "Fortune (Τύχη), too, powerfully helps the delusion, and by the unexpected aid that she sometimes lends, tempts men to venture with inferior means; and this is especially the case with communities, because the stakes played for are the highest, freedom or empire, and when all are acting together, each man irrationally magnifies his own capacity."[45] This betrays how Thucydides sees those who follow Tyche for their own gains; they are usually opportunists of lower intelligence and destined to fail in their pursuits. He finds that "chance . . . simply represents an element which cannot be foretold,"[46] but to follow Tyche or to use her as an excuse for "their own mental incapacity"[47] is reprehensible.

When the first boat is sent to Mitylene to kill all the men and enslave the women and children, Diodotus' call for more leniencies is found to be the more expedient policy. Thucydides points out that the second boat, sent to stop the catastrophe that the first boat is to commit, has the "fortune" (τύχην) of not meeting any winds to impede their progress to the island and also the fortune that those in the first boat were not heading towards this assignment with alacrity. Here, Tyche is implied as being merciful, but again it is the willpower of the men on the second ship, as well as the disdain of the men on the first ship that saves the Mitylenians. Again, the human agent is stronger than the divine, but in this case, Thucydides implies that this is the most fortunate of occurrences.

Demosthenes, in trying to take the Aetolians, is said to have put his trust into the Messenian advice as well as "his fortune" (την τύχη).[48] Yet, this is again an ironic use of "fortune," for, as one finds out in just a few sentences, the best 120 Athenian hoplites meet their demise due to his faith that all will be fine. Again, Thucydides points out that Demosthenes was knowingly lacking in light infantry and dart-men, but moved ahead anyways before Locrian reinforcements arrived, allowing the Aetolians to move up a hill above Aegitium to a strategic advantage.[49] Therefore, if he had just followed more care in maintaining his forces as well as more prudence in action, Thucydides implies, the massacre would have never happened, and Demosthenes could have returned to Athens with pride.

Demosthenes, in Thucydides work, does get another chance, and again Tyche plays her role at the battle. In one of the few times that Thucydides shows any type of excitement, he writes, "Ἀλλόκοτος μεταβολη τύχης!" or "What a bizarre change of Fortune!"[50] However, the Hellenist Richard Crowley translated it as "a strange reversal of the order of things," removing the divine from the vagaries of Fortuna from these events.[51] Thucydides finds that chance has placed the Athenians in Lacedaemon fighting off a seaborne attack from the land. This is truly an odd place for Athens, as it conducts its best warfare at sea. Crowley, however, does not wish to attribute this to the divine. Again, Thucydides gives Tyche her moment in the most glorious of battles. The wording Thucydides again uses implies Tyche's role but does not state it outright. However, the victory at Sphacteria and Pylos rejuvenated the Athenian spirit, as they had just won a battle against Sparta, a polis that was thought to never surrender, in the most unpredictable conditions imaginable by any Greek. This was enough to allow Thucydides to, for once, imply that chance, or Tyche herself, would play her hand in Athenian fortune.

Yet again talk of fortune manifests with the Spartan's appeal for negotiations after this battle. Thucydides implies a character-flaw in Athens that comes to more light by Tyche's hand. The Lacedaemons appeal to Athens to not wish for more good fortune based on this one great victory. Rather, the Athenians are begged to act judiciously.[52] They are reminded that "the prosperity that the city now enjoys, and the accession that it has lately received, must not make you fancy that fortune will be always with you."[53] Yet, the Athenians do show their hubris and request, as they feel that Tyche is with them and that they have a clear upper hand by holding hostages, they want a full surrender from the men on the island as well as Nisaea, Pegae, Troezen, and Achaia. This was to show the character flaw in those who expected Tyche to give more once she gave much, which could also lead, to the Greek mind, to a fall from power. Athens would pay for this.

In Hermocrates' speech, Tyche is used to discern the difference between success and failure from right and wrong, as he points out that "vengeance is not necessarily successful because wrong has been done, or strength sure because it is confident...."[54] What the Hellenist Richard Crawley translates as "the incalculable element in the future"[55] was originally τύχη, a concept that does not lend itself to the rationalism of the nineteenth century. Perhaps that is why this concept is so artfully masked by the translation. But the thought of not being able to account for all future events decided by the whims of Tyche work as a great dissuasion against war for Thucydides as it "frightens us all equally."[56]

Thucydides, in these examples, demonstrates that there is a force greater than man, but ultimately it shall be man that decides the outcome of his efforts. Man's plans may be put asunder, but those same plans, if a man be prudent, wise, and resourceful, can be brought back to fruition and his benefit. Tyche, as powerful as she is, must still yield to the plight and arête of mankind.

However, in Book Six, Thucydides provides us with an interesting new twist on Tyche. Nicias, whilst debating the wisdom of invading Sicily, gives two speeches to dissuade the Athenians, but accomplishes the opposite.[57] Yet, in his second speech, Nicias states, "Fearing this, and knowing that we shall have need of much good counsel and more good fortune—a hard matter for mortal men to aspire to—I wish as far as may be to make myself independent of fortune before sailing, and when I do sail, to be as safe as a strong force can make me."[58] This implies that Tyche is in fact stronger than man, and therefore Nicias feels the need to be as prepared for her as he can be. He also does not, in this statement, shy away from winning her favor. This becomes important in that the conquest of Sicily is faced with difficulties. It becomes a disaster, and Tyche seems to not have had Athens in her favor during that campaign. This makes Hermocrates' words all the more harrowing: "Man can control his own desires, but he cannot likewise control circumstances (τύχη)."[59] This thought of reliance on Tyche for good outcomes is shown in this campaign to be folly; still, the Athenians could not prepare enough it seems to be able to deal with her caprice.

Is it because of Tyche that the Athenians lost the Peloponnesian War? Most likely not, however the inexplicable had to be accounted for. In fact, the use of Tyche as a personification of chance finds itself, ironically, more pervasive in Thucydides' text than that of Herodotus. Yet Thucydides has the reputation for being the more "rational" of the two historians. Though the references to fate are most often in speeches by the main characters of the Peloponnesian War, Thucydides' own references to chance imply Tyche's presence enough to prove that this is one force that is stronger than man's self-determination. However, man has to prepare for her vagaries in order to succeed, which becomes the fatal flaw for the Athenians in Thucydides' history. Those, Thucydides implies in various speeches by the major players of his history, who prepare for the unforeseen manage better than those who act with hubris or haste.

Historiographically, however, searching for Tyche and her influence can become daunting for the researcher and the historian in search of her influence in the Classical Greek histories of Thucydides and Herodotus.[60] Herodotus, though devout in his religion, still believed that man was the master of his own fate. Coincidences showed God's favor, but he was not prone, as Polybius would be over two hundred years later, to attribute the fate of man to anything divine. The gods show favor and also are purported to punish the impious by Herodotus' characters, but in the end, his history is a collection of man creating his own fate. Oracles may have figured heavily in his work, but even this leaves nothing to Tyche. However, in his wishing to leave the divine out of his history, Thucydides finds that the absence of the gods in the fate of man ironically requires Tyche's presence.

For Thucydides, Tyche becomes relatively prominent as the other gods fall silent. He finds in her the impetus for man to strive to prepare, learn, and persevere. Battles are won and lost as she changes a participant's "fortune" and many speeches in his work reference Tyche very obviously. Perhaps this is because "Greek religion was largely practical in orientation...therefore accommodative to the diverse rituals and beliefs of various social strata."[61] To the Greek mind, to remove the gods from human endeavors would leave a practical hole in those unexplained events. To fill this, it would be natural for a Greek, and in this case Thucydides, to turn to Tyche to allow for an understanding of the inexplicable rise and fall of man. With this in mind, it becomes no wonder that Tyche is more predominant in Thucydides than in Herodotus: Herodotus allowed for divine explanation, whereas Thucydides would not. But if man could not be fully attributed to his own fate, Thucydides' practicality demanded that a reason be found. Tyche, therefore, became that reason.

Tyche was meant to be rallied against or courted for her favors. She was sometimes the patron of a city, and randomness was her supposed hallmark. She could make a poor man rich or level a powerful city. She was capricious yet generous. However, Tyche was the goddess of fortune and her presence was simultaneously dreaded and hoped-for. But Tyche's appearance in Herodotus and Thucydides betrays something deeper about human nature: Man will always strive to find order in chaos, and a reason behind every coincidence. Tyche, when no other reason could be found, was a perfect goddess to attribute those events to—especially when the other gods in the pantheon of Greek religion were not utilized. For Herodotus and Thucydides, however, man was still the meter by which all other aspects of life were to be measured, and it was man himself who could dictate the outcome of Tyche's fancies.

Notes

[1] Herodotus *The Histories* 7.10.e.

[2] Hesiod *Theogony* line 360;

[3] Pindar, *The Exant Odes of Pindar,* "For Ergoteles of Himera, Winner of the Long Foot Race." Kindle e-book.

[4] Jerome G. Manis and Bernard N. Meltzer, "Chance in Human Affairs," *Sociological Theory* 12, no. 1 (March, 1994): 46-47.

[5] Polybius *The Complete Histories,* Kindle e-book.

[6] Hesiod, lines 170-210.

[7] Hesiod, lines 336-363.

[8] Kathleen J. Shelton, "Imperial Tyches," *Gesta* 18, no. 1(1979): 29.

[9] Ibid.

[10] Charles Freeman, *Egypt, Greece, and Rome: Civilizations of the Ancient Mediterranean,* 3rd ed. (Oxford: Oxford University Press, 2004), 282.

[11] Herodotus 9.100.

[12] Herodotus 2.50.

[13] Ibid., 2.53.

[14] Ibid., 2.52.

[15] Freeman, 279.

[16] Ernst Breisach, *Historiography: Ancient, Medieval, and Modern* 3rd ed. (Chicago: University of Chicago Press, 2007), 15.

[17] Arnold Toynbee, *Greek Historical Thought* (New York: Mentor, 1952), 199.

[18] H. D. F. Kitto, *The Greeks* (London: Penguin, 1991), 176.

[19] *Dictionary of Greek and Roman Antiquities,* s.v. "Tyche."

[20] Pindar "For Melissos of Thebes, Winner in the Pankration,"Trans. by Ernest Myers, Kindle e-book.

[21] Herodotus, 1.32.

[22] Herodotus, 1.118.

[23] Supposedly Cyrus was exposed to the elements as an infant, but rescued and suckled by a dog. At least, that is the legend that Herodotus relates, his main purpose being to disprove that legend. Herodotus, 1.108-1.122.

[24] Herodotus 1.118.

[25] Herodotus, 1.124. The original Greek is thus: "ὦ παῖ Καμβύσεω, σὲ γὰρ θεοὶ ἐπορῶσι· οὐ γὰρ ἂν κοτὲ ἐς τοσοῦτο τύχης ἀπίκευ· σύ νυν Ἀστυάγεα τὸν σεωυτοῦ φονέα τῖσαι. . ." Again the presence of "fortune" or "luck" is readily discernable in the word "τύχης." Herodotus could have chosen to use μοιρα, or fate, instead.

[26] Herodotus, 1.114-1.118.

[27] Derek Collins, "Nature, Cause, and Agency in Greek Magic," *Transactions of the American Philological Association (1974-)* 133, no. 1 (2003): 19.

[28] Greek version: Herodotus 7.10.d.; Translation of the same text: Herodotus, *The History of Herodotus,* trans. G. C. Macaulay, 7.10.d, Kindle e-book.

[29] Herodotus 9.100-9.101.

[30] Herodotus 8.87-8.88.

[31] J. B. Bury, *The Ancient Greek Historians* (New York: Dover Publications, 1958), 47.

[32] Ibid., 48.

[33] Ibid., 54-60.

[34] Ibid., 60.

[35] J. A. S. Evans, *Herodotus* (Boston: Twane Publishers, 1982), 101.

[36] Bury, 125.

[37] Bresiach, 15.

[38] Ibid., 14-15.

[39] Ibid.

[40] Thucydides *The History of the Peloponnesian War* 1.84.

[41] Thucydides 1.84.

[42] Thucydides 1.140.

[43] Thucydides 1.144.

[44] Thucydides 2.11.

[45] Thucydides 3.45.

[46] Bury, 129.

[47] Ibid., 130.

[48] Thucydides 3.97.

[49] Thucydides 3.97.

[50] Thucydides 4.12. Translation mine.

[51] Thucydides, *The History of the Peloponnesian War,* trans. by Richard Crowley (New York: Barnes & Noble Classics, 2006), 226.

[52] Thucydides 4.17.

[53] Thucydides 4.18.

[54] Thucydides 4.62

[55] Thucydides, *The History of the Peloponnesian War,* trans. by Richard Crowley, (New York: Barnes & Noble Classics, 2006), 251.

[56] Thucydides 4.62.

[57] Thucydides 6.9- 6.24

[58] Thucydides 6.23.

[59] Thucydides 6.78.

[60] Thucydides, *The History of the Peloponnesian War,* trans. by Richard Crowley, (New York: Barnes & Noble Classics, 2006), 179n.

[61] Joseph M. Brant, "Intellectuals and Religion in Ancient Greece: Notes on a Weberian Theme," *The British Journal of Sociology* 37, no. 2 (June, 1986): 280.

Bibliography

Brant, Joseph M. "Intellectuals and Religion in Ancient Greece: Notes on a Weberian Theme." *The British Journal of Sociology* 37, no. 2 (June, 1986): 269-296.

Breisach, Ernst. *Historiography: Ancient, Medieval, and Modern.* 3rd ed. Chicago and London: University of Chicago Press, 2007.

Bury, J. B. *The Ancient Greek Historians.* New York: Dover Publications, 1958.

Collins, Derek. "Nature, Cause, and Agency in Greek Magic." *Transactions of the American Philological Association (1974-)* 133, no. 1 (2003): 19.

Evans, J. A. S. *Herodotus.* Boston: Twayne Publishers, 1982.

Freeman, Charles. *Egypt, Greece, and Rome: Civilizations of the Ancient Mediterranean.* 3rd ed. Oxford: Oxford University Press, 2004.

Herodotus. *The History of Herodotus.* Translated by G. C. Macaulay. London: Macmillan & Co., Ltd., 1914. Kindle e-book.

Herodotus. *The Histories.* Vol. 3 of *Bibliotheca Classica.* London: Whittaker & Co., 1854.

Herodotus. *The Histories.* Translated by Aubrey de Selincourt. Rev. ed. London: Penguin Classics. 2003.

Hesiod. *Theogony, Works and Days, and Shield.* Translated by Apostolos N. Athanassakis. Baltimore and London: Johns Hopkins University Press, 1983.

Kitto, H. D. F. *The Greeks.* London: Penguin, 1991.

Manis, Jerome G. and Bernard N. Meltzer. "Chance in Human Affairs," *Sociological Theory* 12, no. 1 (March, 1994): 45-56.

Pindar. *The Extant Odes of Pindar.* Translated and edited by Ernest Myers. Kindle e-book.

Shelton, Kathleen J. "Imperial Tyches." *Gesta* 18, no. 1(1979): 27-38.

Thucydides. *Πελοποννεσιακος Πολεμος* [Peloponnesian Wars]. 1909. Kindle e-book.

Thucydides. *The History of the Peloponnesian War.* Translated by Richard Crowley. New York: Barnes & Noble Classics, 2006.

Toynbee, Arnold. *Greek Historical Thought.* New York: Mentor, 1952.

The Conscience of a Nation: The Social Work of Jane Addams In Chicago's Immigrant Communities

Susanne Watts

Give me your tired, your poor,
Your huddled masses yearning to breathe free,
The wretched refuse of your teeming shore.
Send these, the homeless, tempest-tost to me,
I lift my lamp beside the golden door!

These well-known lines of Emma Lazarus' poem on the Statue of Liberty served as an invitation to millions of immigrants during the Gilded Age, hoping to find a better life for themselves and their families. Immigration to the United States during the last four decades of the nineteenth century numbered over thirteen million, with more than eighty percent coming from Europe.[1] The majority of these immigrants settled in urban areas that promised abundant work in factories. These jobs were indicative of America's industrial expansion, and most immigrants "came into the very bottom of American urban industrial society."[2] Settling in overcrowding city neighborhoods, living conditions were appalling. Thus, Emma Lazarus' words came to describe immigrants' actual working as well as living conditions in their new home country more so than the allure of the Promised Land. The plight of working-class immigrants soon caught the attention of middle-class social reformers. Social visionaries like Jane Addams sought to use social reform to improve the lives of poor working-class immigrants. Jane Addams believed in an individual's obligation to help the community. Through her visionary pioneer work, she provided invaluable social services to the immigrant poor, and brought their plight onto the public stage. Her work at Hull House was influential in advocating social reform and extending social services at the local and state level, and would eventually influence federal legislation. Hull House also facilitated an exchange not only between the social classes but also between different ethnicities. The services Hull House provided helped immigrants assimilate into American culture and society.

Jane Addams was born on September 6, 1860 in Cedarville, Illinois. Her father, John Huy Addams, was a man of strong moral convictions, and committed to the principles of social justice. This clearly had an impact on Jane and her future work. She acknowledged, "It was this cord which not only held fast my supreme affections, but also first drew me into the moral concerns of life."[3] While her father supported women's suffrage, and "respected his daughter's ability to think and to make up her own mind," he was opposed to Jane's future educational plans of earning a Bachelor of Arts and attending medical school.[4] Instead, Addams attended Rockford Female Seminary and graduated in 1881 with a collegiate certificate. In her senior essay, she stressed the importance of "the educated woman to apply her gift of intuition to seek social reforms and to not restrict herself and her sympathies to the home and child-drearing."[5] Having been denied the opportunity to further her academic education, Addams set off with family members in 1883 to travel extensively in Europe. It was during this trip that she first experienced the poor neighborhoods of London. The sight of utter poverty and failure of society to provide a minimum amount of basic necessities as well as human dignity, left Addams very disturbed, feeling a deep sense of failure.[6] This experience would provide the impetus for Addams to address the call for women's involvement in social reforms, and thus bring purpose and meaning to her senior essay.

While Jane Addams had a vague idea of what she wanted to do to not only give her life purpose but also do meaningful work for society, she was "convinced that it would be a good thing to rent a house in a part of the city where many primitive and actual needs are found."[7] Realizing that other educated middle-class women experienced a similar sense of disconnect, she envisioned to establish a community that would immerse itself into the life of the working class. The idea of establishing a settlement house where young women like her would live among the working-class poor was shaped after her encounter with the poor in London during her first European trip. With a clearer picture and purpose, Jane set off for her second trip to Europe in 1887, this time with her longtime friend, Ellen Gates Starr. During this trip, they would visit Toynbee Hall in London, the world's first settlement house, to gain insight into the daily operations and to experience what they could expect in starting a similar venture in the United States.

Toynbee Hall opened its doors in 1884 as a "University Settlement in East London, where a small community of 'settlers' could live and work amongst the local people."[8] Its founder, Samuel Barnett, hoped to attract young college-educated men to live and work in the impoverished area of East London in order to improve the lives of its poor working-class citizens. Toynbee Hall offered a variety of services and classes to the community by addressing the basic educational needs of the poor. It offered classes in basic math, reading, and writing free of charge. What made Toynbee Hall revolutionary was its focus to develop "personal relationships between rich and poor in order to break down the class divisions."[9] This emphasis on sharing mutual experiences between different social classes was another important aspect Jane Addams would incorporate into her settlement house philosophy. Toynbee Hall was supposed to function as a place that brought different social classes together through education. Barnett was a strong proponent of providing access to culture to everybody, stating, "everyone should have access to art, music, literature and learning, not just a wealthy or University-educated elite."[10] While his ideas were certainly revolutionary and commendable, they also revealed a paternalistic attitude common of the affluent class at the time. In the eyes of most middle-class social reformers, the poor needed their work and expertise in order to improve their lives. However, the concept of the settlement house was groundbreaking as it exposed educated middle-class men and women to the harsh realities of living in poor neighborhoods.

Toynbee Hall represented what Jane Addams envisioned for her own settlement house idea. Addams wanted to implement the goal of the settlement movement by bringing the rich and poor to live more closely together in an interdependent community. In order to achieve that goal, she would establish her settlement house in a poor urban area to alleviate poverty by providing needed services, as well as help the working-class poor to improve their lives. In contrast to Toynbee Hall, Addams wanted her settlement house to focus on working with immigrants. She chose to settle in Chicago, as Ellen Gates Starr was already teaching at the Kirkland School.[11] One of the more difficult tasks was to find a suitable immigrant neighborhood and a suitable property in the community. After months of searching, Addams and Starr found a diverse immigrant neighborhood in Chicago's West Side, in the Nineteenth Ward. The neighborhood was nearly all immigrants, with over eighteen nationalities represented.[12] Not only did the Nineteenth Ward consist of a very diverse working-class population, it was also home to a variety of manufacturing and business establishments. Thus, the neighborhood Addams and Starr chose was in its truest sense a working-class neighborhood, where its inhabitants lived and worked. It also meant that the more affluent classes, especially women, had very little to no contact with the immigrants. They were truly living in segregated and separated communities. Addams' settlement house was to change this by inviting middle-class women residents to "learn to know the people and understand them and their way of life."[13] Addams and Starr's settlement house, named Hull House after the previous owner, Charles J. Hull, opened its doors on September 19, 1889 to begin its work creating a community that would benefit both its middle-class residents as well as the neighborhood's working-class immigrants.

Aside from emphasizing the mutual benefits the work of Hull House aimed to achieve, Addams hoped that Hull House would be a place of mutual exchanges between the social classes, where everyone could learn from each other. Her mission was to not only offer immediate help to improve the immigrants' lives but to also provide them with an opportunity of possible long-term economic advancement. Similar to Barnett, Addams also believed that educated middle-class women were best suited to facilitate this goal. However, Addams also realized that in order to achieve this goal Hull House workers had to meet their neighbors in their own homes. Striving to effectively help the neighborhood, Hull House needed to play an active part in the immigrants' daily lives. Thus, Hull House's mission was based on three ethical principles: "to teach by example, to practice cooperation, and to practice social democracy, that is, egalitarian, or democratic, social relations across class lines."[14] While there were other organizations that tried to ameliorate the living conditions of the working-class via private social reform movements, very few actually lived and worked directly in the neighborhoods of those they helped. Hull House in that regard was a groundbreaking establishment, as it was located within the community it aimed to serve, and its residents went into the neighborhood to work directly with its people. Applying Hull House's principles, "Addams and Starr made getting to know people the first order of the day," much to the confusion of their new neighbors. The neighborhood was suspicious of the intentions of these two middle-class white women.[15] In applying Hull House principles in their daily interactions, Addams and other residents slowly gained the confidence of the neighborhood. The so-called friendly visit to immigrants' homes provided invaluable information to Hull House in assessing the immediate needs of the neighborhood. Addams hoped these visits "also functioned to uplift and alleviate the sufferings of the poor through the ameliorative effects of class contact," which brought different social classes together.[16] Again, there is an implied paternalistic attitude that the poor needed the middle-class as an uplifting example in order to overcome their economic poverty. It is no surprise then that Hull House's immigrant neighbors viewed its work at first with suspicion.

The neighborhood around Hull House was unique in that it consisted of a very diverse population. The Nineteenth Ward's inhabitants represented eighteen different nationalities. This was not surprising, as Chicago was attracting immigrants due to its importance as a major economic center during the late nineteenth century. Chicago's "meatpacking, liquor, steel and iron, clothing, railroad car, and agricultural machinery industries were thriving," as it concentrated a diverse selection of the new economy's industries.[17] Chicago's thriving economy attracted immigrants, however the majority of these new economy jobs were in unskilled labor, which placed the great majority of immigrants at the bottom social class of the urban industrial society. In terms of population, the 1890 "United States Census revealed that of Chicago's 1.1 million people an astonishing 855,000 were either foreign born or their American-born children."[18] Thus, Hull House established itself in one of the city's most ethnically diverse and economically depressed areas. Even though the neighborhood was distinctly diverse, immigrants kept to their own ethnic neighborhoods, segregating themselves.

Statistical information collected by Hull House residents confirmed that immigrants "are more or less intermingled, but a decided tendency to drift into little colonies is apparent."[19]

Addams and Starr had wanted to focus on an immigrant neighborhood with mostly German and French inhabitants because they had spent considerable time in these countries during their travels to Europe, spoke the language, and were familiar with the peoples' culture and customs. However, reality in the Nineteenth Ward neighborhood was different, as immigration during the later decades of the nineteenth century attracted mostly immigrants from southern and eastern Europe. According to *Hull-House Maps and Papers,* "The Italians, the Russian and Polish Jews, and the Bohemians lead in numbers and importance. The Irish control the polls; while the Germans, although they make up more than a third of Chicago's population, are not very numerous in this neighborhood."[20] However, within ten years of the first publication of the neighborhood's ethnic composition, the *American Journal of Sociology* reported that Italians now composed seventy-two percent of the community, while the Greeks made up thirteen percent, and the rest "divided among twenty-seven different nationalities."[21] Thus, the neighborhood around Hull House was in constant flux, and Hull House residents had to be flexible in trying to assess the needs of the individual ethnic immigrant communities. It was not a "one size fits all" approach, as the immigrant communities perceived Jane Addams and Hull House in different ways, depending on the already established immigrant communities' social organizations. Hull House succeeded in building and maintaining a positive relationship with the Greek community, which resulted in a concentration of "the Greek community's social and cultural activities" in Hull House.[22] However, due to the Catholic Church's influence on the Italian community, Hull House was not able to connect with poor Italian immigrants.

In effect, Hull House was considered a "major competitor for the souls of Italian children."[23] Nevertheless, the appalling living conditions in the Nineteenth Ward allowed Hull House to connect with all of its immigrant neighbors by working to improve their lives.

The overall conditions of the Nineteenth Ward did not discriminate or segregate by ethnicity. The neighborhood presented Hull House with problems that needed to be addressed immediately in order to create safer living conditions. As mentioned earlier, the Nineteenth Ward was a true working-class neighborhood where people lived and worked. People often worked in the same place they also lived. This created various hazards due to overcrowding, unsanitary conditions, and the lack of effective city services. Many of the tenement houses were in dilapidated conditions, lacking adequate sanitation, sufficient ventilation, and were generally not kept up by mostly absent landlords. The main problem in the neighborhood was overcrowding, which exacerbated the unsanitary conditions. City services were almost non-existent, as "the streets are inexpressibly dirty, the number of schools inadequate, sanitary legislation unenforced, the street lighting bad, the paving miserable and altogether lacking in the alleys and smaller streets, and the stables foul beyond description. Hundreds of houses are unconnected with the street sewer."[24] Addams realized that these conditions represented a great disadvantage for the immigrants' advancement. The living conditions in the Nineteenth Ward made it nearly impossible for its inhabitants to live healthy, and avoid often-deadly diseases. The appalling conditions were also detrimental to the general welfare of the neighborhood, and adversely affected the immigrants' assimilation into American society. Poor immigrants' neighborhoods around the country were often considered a by-product of unrestrained immigration, and blamed on a foreign immigrant culture that was unwilling to be Americanized.

Through Hull House's work, Jane Addams tried to convince the middle-class and political leaders that the immigrants' living and working environment, and not his or her character were responsible for the economic and social plight. If immigrants were presented with favorable conditions in their environment then they would easier identify with their new country. Therefore, it was important to Hull House to offer services that would help immigrants to assimilate into American culture and society. In order for immigrants to be fully integrated into American society, they had to become a part of all aspects of American life and society. Hull House and its residents were there to guide and educate its immigrant neighbors without any preconceived notions and prejudices. The aspect of treating immigrants as equals was very important to Addams, as it was an important aspect of the principle of social democracy. For Addams, "social democracy meant eliminating social, national, and cultural barriers among newcomers and between them and native-born Americans."[25] Therefore, although the work at Hull House could be regarded as charity work to provide immediate support for the immigrants' plight, it would also serve as a long-term support system in order to bring the different social classes together. In that regard, the purpose of Hull House was not considered to simply relieve poverty "but rather an opportunity to realize the radically democratic potentials of its cross-cultural exchanges for both the middle-class settlement house workers and the community."[26] Hull House served as a place where people from all social classes and ethnic backgrounds could come together, and connect with each other to build a more just and a more social democracy.

The concept of assimilation also implied that immigrants could not stay segregated in their own ethnic communities within the Nineteenth Ward. Hull House intended to bring immigrants from different backgrounds together by offering a variety of classes and clubs, as well as opening its doors to ethnic associations. The educational aspects of Hull House, as well as its civic and social community engagements, were "but differing manifestations of the attempt to socialize democracy, as is the very existence of the Settlement itself."[27] Hull House's main purpose was still to serve its immediate community by providing services that would ameliorate the neighborhood's most pressing needs. Over the years, Hull House extended its services, again showing flexibility in adapting to the changing needs of its neighbors. Some of the most practical services that had an immediate impact on the community were day care, kindergarten, after school care and clubs for children, a coffeehouse and kitchen to serve inexpensive meals, offices to assist people with employment, a medical clinic, and a lodging house for women.[28] In order to truly assimilate immigrants into American society, Hull House offered a variety of educational services, which were very popular. Hull House offered concerts, had its own orchestra and children's choir, housed an art gallery to expose immigrants to fine culture, and offered college extension courses, which "introduced newcomers to Western-American culture and created opportunities for individual immigrants to gain higher education in the professions or to develop their intellectual talents to prepare them to gain higher education."[29] While the educational classes helped realize Addams' ideal of bringing different immigrant ethnicities together, the social clubs were often separated by ethnicity. However, the educational and cultural goals of Hull House at times clashed with the immigrants' ideas and culture, and forced Hull House to adjust its activities. In the case of the Italians, Hull House "shifted the emphasis from educational and cultural programs to sports, dancing, playing, and crafts."[30] Jane Addams realized that assimilation could not be forced on the immigrants. Instead of alienating a major part of the community, Hull House adjusted to their needs. By doing so, Addams acknowledged that in order to achieve a true sense of community one had to understand each other's way of life and learn through mutual experiences. This experience would not have been possible outside of Hull House's environment and mission. Overall, Hull House helped the assimilation process by building a bridge between immigrants' past and present.

The work of Jane Addams and Hull House brought the plight of America's immigrant working-class onto the public stage. Middle-class reformers like Addams realized that the upper social classes had an obligation to work towards a more social and just democracy. This meant they had to experience the immigrants' life to a certain extent. By establishing a settlement house in a diverse immigrant neighborhood, Addams was able to directly ameliorate the most immediate needs of the community and also provided long-term studies that were used to enact much-needed social reforms. Hull House provided important services to the immigrant community by instituting "programs that would promote ethnic mixing and further the process of assimilation."[31] In that regard, Jane Addams' mission to create an exchange between the social classes and different ethnicities served as a model to help immigrants assimilate into American society. By practicing cooperation, teaching by example, and trying to create egalitarian social relationships across class lines, Jane Addams not only gave hope to the "huddled masses" of Chicago's Nineteenth Ward but also provided them with educational and social opportunities to find the Promised Land in America.

Notes

[1] Roger Daniels, "The Immigrant Experience in the Gilded Age," in *The Gilded Age*, ed. by Charles W. Calhoun (Lanham: Rowman & Littlefield Publishers, 2007), 78-79.

[2] Ibid., 87.

[3] Jane Addams, *Twenty Years at Hull House* (New York, 1910), 26 (Project Gutenberg, 1998), EPUB, accessed November 11, 2013, http://www.gutenberg.org/ebooks/1325.

[4] Louise W. Knight, *Citizen: Jane Addams and the Struggle for Democracy* (Chicago: University of Chicago Press, 2005), 81, Ebrary Reader, accessed December 21, 2013, http://site.ebrary.com/lib/apus/docDetail.action?docID=10265951.

[5] Ibid., 123.

[6] Ibid., 150.

[7] Addams, *Twenty Years at Hull House,* 117.

[8] Jo Till, "Icons of Toynbee Hall - Samuel Barnett," Toynbee Hall, accessed December 15, 2013, http://www.toynbeehall.org.uk/data/files/About_Toynbee_Hall/Barnett_low_res.pdf.

[9] Ibid.

[10] Ibid.

[11] Knight, *Citizen: Jane Addams and the Struggle for Democracy,* 196.

[12] Ibid., 211.

[13] Ibid., 198.

[14] Ibid., 199.

[15] Ibid., 220.

[16] James B. Salazar, *Bodies of Reform: The Rhetoric of Character in Gilded Age America* (New York: NYU Press, 2010), 222, Ebrary Reader, accessed December 21, 2013, http://site.ebrary.com/lib/apus/docDetail.action?docID=10420306.

[17] Knight, *Citizen: Jane Addams and the Struggle for Democracy,* 203.

[18] Melvin G. Holli, "Hull House and the Immigrants," Immigrants, Illinois Periodicals Online, Northern Illinois University Libraries, accessed December 15, 2013, http://www.lib.niu.edu/2003/iht1010323.html.

[19] *Hull-House Maps and Papers, a Presentation of Nationalities and Wages in a congested District of Chicago, together with Comments and Essays on Problems growing out of the Social Conditions* (New York: T. Y. Crowell, 1895), 39 (American Libraries), EPUB, accessed November 11, 2013, https://archive.org/details/hullhousemapspap00newy.

[20] Ibid., 40.

[21] Natalie Walker, "Chicago Housing Conditions. X. Greeks and Italians in the Neighborhood of Hull House," *American Journal of Sociology* 21, no. 3 (November 1915): 290, accessed November 15, 2013, http://www/jstor.org/stable/27638971.

[22] Rivka Shpak Lissak, *Pluralism & Progressives - Hull House and the New Immigrants, 1890-1919* (Chicago: University of Chicago Press, 1989), 104.

[23] Ibid., 100.

[24] Addams, *Twenty Years at Hull House,* 131-132.

[25] Lissak, *Pluralism & Progressives,* 25.

[26] Salazar, *Bodies of Reform,* 229.

[27] Addams, *Twenty Years at Hull House,* 518.

[28] Dorothea Moore, "A Day at Hull House," *American Journal of Sociology* 2, no. 5 (March 1897): 631-634, accessed November 15, 2013, http://www.jstor.org/stable/2761647.

[29] Lissak, *Pluralism & Progressives,* 47.

[30] Ibid., 120.

[31] Shelton Stromquist, *Re-inventing "The People"* (Chicago: University of Chicago Press, 2006), 149.

Bibliography

Addams, Jane. *Twenty Years at Hull House.* New York, 1910. Project Gutenberg, 1998. EPUB. Accessed November 11, 2013, http://www.gutenberg.org/ebooks/1325.

Daniels, Roger. "The Immigrant Experience in the Gilded Age." In *The Gilded Age,* edited by Charles W. Calhoun, 75-99. Lanham: Rowman & Littlefield Publishers, 2007.

Holli, Melvin G. "Hull House and the Immigrants." Immigrants. Illinois Periodicals Online, Northern Illinois University Libraries. Accessed December 15, 2013, http://www.lib.niu.edu/2003/iht1010323.html.

Hull-House Maps and Papers, a Presentation of Nationalities and Wages in a congested District of Chicago, together with Comments and Essays on Problems growing out of the social Conditions. New York: T. Y. Crowell, 1895. American Libraries. EPUB. Accessed November 11, 2013, http://archive.org/details/hullhousemaps pap00newy.

Knight, Louise W. *Citizen: Jane Addams and the Struggle for Democracy.* Chicago: University of Chicago Press, 2005. Ebrary Reader. Accessed December 21, 2013, http://site.ebrary.com/lib/apus/docDetail.action?docID=10265951.

Lazarus, Emma. "The New Colossus." The Statue of Liberty and Ellis Island Website. Accessed December 20, 2013, http://www.libertystatepark.com/emma.htm.

Lissak, Rivka Shpak. *Pluralism & Progressives - Hull House and the New Immigrants, 1890-1919.* Chicago: University of Chicago Press, 1989.

Moore, Dorothea. "A Day at Hull House." *American Journal of Sociology* 2, no. 5 (March 1897): 629-642. Accessed November 15, 2013, http://www.jstor.org/stable/2761647.

Salazar, James B. *Bodies of Reform: The Rhetoric of Character in Gilded Age America.* New York: NYU Press, 2010. Ebrary Reader. Accessed December 21, 2013, http://site.ebrary.com/lib/apus/docDetail.action?docID=10420306.

Stromquist, Shelton. *Re-inventing "The People."* Chicago: University of Chicago Press, 2006.

Till, Jo. "Icons of Toynbee Hall - Samuel Barnett." Toynbee Hall. Accessed December 15, 2013, http://www.toynbeehall.org.uk/data/files/About_Toynbee_Hall/Barnett_low_res.pdf.

Walker, Natalie. "Chicago Housing Conditions. X. Greeks and Italians in the Neighborhood of Hull House." *American Journal of Sociology* 21, no. 3 (November 1915): 285-316. Accessed November 15, 2013, http://www.jstor.org/stable/27638971.

Conquerors and Conquered: Early Perspectives of the Battle of Hastings

Matthew Hudson

On 14 October 1066, the balance of power on the British Isles shifted when William the Bastard defeated Harold II, the last Saxon king of England, on the field of battle at Hastings. The outcome of a battle or the succession of one ruler from another is easy to define and catalog. However, when the reason for and interpretation of the event become the focus, then the voice of the historian may define the next generation's understanding and perception of the world created by the outcome. The historiography of the Battle of Hastings provides a glimpse into the mind of those writing the history. The ethics, economics, and social norms of the historians are presented to the reader as their work interprets the past. The generation that fought at Hastings and the generations which followed provided future generations with the root system which supported a tree of knowledge. The world in which Hastings occurred can be heard within these voices of conquerors and conquered.

The concept of divine will played a major role in the Middle Ages. The Anglo-Saxon versions of the invasion spoke of divine punishment, while the Norman versions exalted divine retribution and worldly valor. The most visual and well-known history of the event, the Bayeux Tapestry (c. 1080), is wrapped in mystery. The patron, or patrons, of the tapestry can only be speculated upon. Prominent early sources concerning Hastings included *The Anglo-Saxon Chronicle*, the pro-Norman works of Wace, and the Anglo-Norman interpretations of William of Malmesbury and Orderic Vitalis. The histories of the Battle of Hastings offered in the decades following the conflict offer the modern world more than just the events of the day; they provide a glimpse into how a story may be told differently based on the point of view of the storyteller.

The Anglo-Saxon Chronicle told of a nation of people that was paying for sins and the misdeeds of their leaders. Captured within the early historiography of the conquest of England was a tale of missteps, retribution, and harbingers of doom. Coincidently, the year 1066 witnessed the return of Halley's Comet. Man had long viewed comets as the harbingers of doom. *The Anglo-Saxon Chronicle,* originally commissioned by Alfred the Great around 890, compiled the works of many church educated authors that spanned generations of effort. Indeed, there are chronicles originating from monasteries around the kingdom reporting simultaneously upon the events of the same years. Among the events of the year 1066, it was reported that "all over England such a token seen as no man ever saw before."[1] The conquered Saxons discovered a world in which they became second-class citizens. Unlike the majority of the Viking raids from the previous centuries, this new group of invaders sought more than possessions, wealth, or a mere foothold on the isle. The Normans came to rule, and altered the culture and kingdom of England in the process.

One telling feature of the Saxon account was the manner in which the combatants were identified: King Harold and Earl William, King Edward's cousin. Although clearly written after the events of the battle, the Saxons still viewed Harold's claim as legitimate — referring to Harold as King and William as the lower station of earl. Religion played a vital role in eleventh century Europe, and if a king was crowned by someone who had been excommunicated, that king's reign would be invalidated. The Worcester version of the *Chronicle* confirmed the legitimacy of Harold due to his having been crowned by Ealdred, archbishop of York; conversely, Norman sources claimed that Harold was crowned by Stigand, archbishop of Canterbury, who had been excommunicated.[2]

The Saxon account described Harold as gathering a large force, but William "came against him unawares, ere his army was collected; but the king, nevertheless, very hardly encountered him with the men that would support him."[3] The Normans won the day "as God granted them for the sins of the nation."[4] The Saxons delayed submission to the victorious William. It was believed that God wanted nothing better for the sins of the Saxons than Norman lords harassing the populace of England and causing increasing levels of misery. The *Chronicle* delivered a religious morality tale in its effort to explain the loss of Saxon England. In the Middle Ages, the losing side of a conflict or a population suffering plague viewed the misery as divine punishment. Harold's lack of his full forces and having fought in a major battle at Stamford Bridge just a few weeks before Hastings could rationalize the hard-fought loss described by the Saxons. But that rationalization always came second to divine punishment. For the Saxons, defeat was a predestined divine punishment that neither tactics nor size of force could overcome.

Not surprisingly, the details of the very same battle described by the vanquished as divine punishment were viewed as divine will by the victorious Normans. Often performed by entertainers known as *jongleurs,* songs of heroic deeds and lineage, *chansons de geste*, enjoyed immense popularity during the Norman era and were often centered on the age of Charlemagne. A sense of the importance of these songs can be gained by noting that the *Domesday Book* (1086) mentioned William's *jongleur*, Berdic, by name, and told of lands given to him as reward for service. "In Normandy, a country with a resurgent aristocracy advancing from conquest to conquest, one of the strongest influences was the sense of lineage; the intense interest in family history was fostered by *chansons* in court or castle, and by narrative charters, recording the ancestry of founders in religious houses."[5] Ascribed to Guy, bishop of Amiens, the *Carmen de Hastingae*

Proelio became the *chansons* related to the battle.

The notions of heroic acts and divine justification were found in the writings of the Normans in reference to the conquest of Saxon England. William of Poitiers, personal chaplain of William the Conqueror, wrote of Harold's sister Edith, wife of King Edward, validating that Edward had wished William become ruler of England. William of Poitiers called Harold a tyrannical ruler and chastised his usurpation of the throne; moreover, he made the claim that the Conquest freed the English from slavery and tyranny.[6] The main argument for Harold's treachery descended from the Norman assertion as seen in the Bayeux Tapestry that Harold swore an oath of fealty to William while in Normandy on a mission from Edward. William of Poitiers's account demonstrates the danger of trusting those authors who were too close to the historical actors, and the biased nature that lies within man's desire to justify his patrons.

An important Norman source of the events of the invasion was Wace (c. 1115- c. 1183), a Norman poet, who wrote in the Norman tradition of songs of heroic deeds and lineage. This could be seen within his two works: *Roman de Brut* (1150-1155), which was more a romance than a history, and *Roman de Rou* (1160- c. 1174), which detailed the greatness of the Norman dukes and the subsequent conquest of England. Wace described that Edward, on his death bed, warned the Saxons that he had promised England to his nephew William despite the desires of the English aristocracy to have Harold rule them. Wace described William as trying to reason with Harold by reminding him of the oath made by Harold in Normandy and by offering to fight in single combat for the throne, but "Harold said he would do neither; he would neither perform his covenant, nor put the matter in judgment, nor would he meet him and fight body to body."[7] Wace portrayed the two sides the night before the battle in stark contrast; the Saxons were depicted as drunkards and the Normans as pious and penitent.[8] While, on the surface, this may be construed as a vindication of the Saxon account of divine punishment, the Saxons never questioned Harold's right to the throne; the Saxon account also did not mention any specific sins or drunken behavior. The Normans sought to present the divine justice and right of rule that legitimized their conquest, and were more specific in their criticisms of the conquered than the Saxons were in self-reflection.

The Norman Conquest transformed England in numerous ways. William divided the lands of England among those who fought alongside him. The Normans also brought religious reform across the English Channel. As with any influx of new people into an area, marriages between the cultures were consummated and the Anglo-Norman world was born. "Some Saxon landholders adapted themselves to the requirements of Norman fighting; there was inter-marriage with the invaders, and the remodeling of the church re-spected most of the ancient ecclesiastical endowments but chan-neled them to different recipients."[9] As England changed and two cultures began the slow merger into one, so did the historiography. The *Anglo-Saxon Chronicle* gradually faded into oblivion around 1154. The Norman accounts of bravery remained; however, a new breed of historian grew within these accounts of bravery. The new histori-ans of Anglo-Norman England often descended from a mixed herit-age of both Norman and Saxon. Yet, the historiography continued to seek divine providence in the outcome of the conflict. William built a church on the site of his victory over Harold and encouraged the ecclesiastical reform within England. The blending of the two cultures and reform within the churches and monasteries of Eng-land provided a new version of the Battle of Hastings to be written – a version that found the divine vindication of the Norman victory, yet managed to provide dignity to the defeated Saxons.

William of Malmesbury (c.1095-1143) contributed to the new Anglo-Norman histories written by those of both Saxon and Norman blood, his mother being a Saxon and his father a Norman. His interpretation walked the fine line of observing the positives in Norman England while longing to connect to the Saxon history of England. William saw the English church pre-1066 as too secular and praised the Norman influence in revitalizing the church. William of Malmesbury acknowledged William of Normandy as Edward's chosen heir; however, he also granted Harold praise by speaking of a sound and just ability to rule. "Still, not to conceal the truth, Harold would have governed the kingdom with prudence and with courage, in the character he had assumed, had he undertaken it lawfully."[10] William of Malmesbury also attempted to be fair and honest with his approach to William the Conqueror. "For my part, as the blood of either people flows in my veins, I shall steer a middle course: where I am certified of his good deeds, I shall openly proclaim them; his bad conduct I shall touch upon lightly and sparingly, though as not so as to conceal it; so that neither shall my narrative be condemned as false, nor will I brand that man with ignominious censure, almost the whole of whose actions may be reasonably excused, if not commended."[11] William of Malmesbury represented the noble efforts of an impartial historiography of the events at Hastings; however, the political landscape within England in the generations after the battle still did not allow for a truly neutral assessment.

William of Malmesbury sought to correct the erroneous accounts of Hastings that he found in both Saxon and Norman histories. William, like many of those writing in Anglo-Norman England, portrayed Harold as an opportunistic usurper. While he did maintain that Harold was suitable for the throne, William supported the Norman claim to England. He wrote that the inflation in numbers of the Saxon army, which he described as prevalent in Norman accounts, did not increase the glory of the Norman Conquest, but instead it diminished it through its inaccuracy.[12] William's account also mentioned how the Saxon will to fight died with Harold. "The effect of war in this affair was trifling; it was brought about by the secret and wonderful counsel of God: since the Angles never again, in any general battle, made struggle for liberty, as if the ... strength [of] England had fallen with Harold, who certainly might and ought to pay the penalty of his perfidy, even though it were at the hands of the most unwarlike people."[13] William's assessment was not meant to belittle the Normans but to speak of the tenacity of a brave, yet small, army of Saxons defending their homeland. His indication of the Norman people as unwarlike was meant to show them as just and not belligerent conquerors. Yet, the notion of Normans being unwarlike was contrary to the spirit of the popular *chansons*. William of Malmesbury, though, offered the positive and negative from both Saxons and Normans.

Another of the Anglo-Norman historians and a contemporary of William of Malmesbury was Orderic Vitalis (1075-1142). Like William, Orderic was a monk. He wrote during a period of great contention. Succession questions had yet to be decided for the manner in which the kingdom and the duchy of Normandy would be divided. After William decided on how to divide his territory, he lived to regret it when his oldest son rebelled against him in an attempt to control all of William's land. Orderic painted a Norman picture with his words on the events of the year 1066. In his account of the Conquest, Orderic saw Harold as the perjurer and William as the liberator of the English. His attempt to provide a true history became entangled with the Norman love of the *chansons*. "How quickly elements taken from them might creep into the accounts of eye-witnesses and so into the pages of serious history appears repeatedly in Orderic's work."[14] Orderic considered Saxon England to be headed toward ruin and the Normans as the great saviors and reformers. "The Normans, although they may have been warlike, troublemaking, ambitious, and deceitful, reformed the English monasteries and upgraded the church on the isle; such sacred and moral considerations must prevail in judgment of past events."[15] Orderic, like William of Malmesbury, had a Norman father and an English mother, however Orderic wrote less of Saxon virtue than William. The Anglo-Norman histories existed as a more honest account of events than of those directly involved in the conflict, but the background of the individual still influenced the interpretation.

Housed in Bayeux, France and commissioned by an unknown patron, the Bayeux Tapestry is the most visual source of the events of the year 1066. The tapestry was likely commissioned by Bishop Odo of Bayeux (c.1030 – 1097) and crafted by Anglo-Saxon artisans in Kent. Alternate patrons could have been Count Eustace of Boulogne (c. 1020 – 1087), another nephew of Edward the Confessor, as well as the tapestry being created as a gift to Odo from the monks of St. Augustine. As mentioned, numerous versions of *The Anglo-Saxon Chronicle* were written and St. Augustine's abbey was one of the locations for this venture. The tapestry presents an intriguing mixture of historiography. A Norman or French patron commissioned a tapestry illustrating the glory of the conquest which in turn was then crafted by those who had been conquered. It is valuable to note that Harold is referred to as 'Harold Rex' in the tapestry's depiction of his accession to the throne, which does not present him in the light of a usurper. Throughout the images portrayed on the Bayeux Tapestry, the viewer becomes empowered to interpret the scene as one pleases. If, as the saying goes, a picture is worth a thousand words, then the tapestry becomes the most voluminous tome on the topic. "The truth behind Harold's mission, and with it King Edward's crucial wishes towards the end of his reign, was recorded at St. Augustine's not, on this occasion, in ink scratched upon parchment but with colorful stitches pierced through white linen cloth."[16] The early chronicles did not mention the manner of Harold's death at Hastings; however, the tapestry shows death coming from an arrow to the eye – possibly the first mention of the cause of death. "The story first appears, or seems to appear, in the Bayeux tapestry; it was first recorded in writing in the otherwise unimportant account of the battle by Baudri of Bourgueil in 1099."[17] It may be impossible to know how the arrow story came about. The tapestry displays a scene of an arrow and one blow from an advancing knight striking Harold. It seems logical that the images of the tapestry influenced the written records that followed.

While the tapestry portrays a vivid account of the actions between Harold and William, it does not give the whole story. "Its pictorial story of Harold and William and the events leading up to and including the Battle of Hastings is a historic treasure of authentic eleventh century detail such as dress and armor and weaponry, but what it tells of Harold is open to serious question."[18] While the picture paints a thousand words, the words come from the viewer's own interpretation. Motives and opportunities of those involved in the events are lost in the viewing of the tapestry. Moreover, the images chosen in the eleventh century will not have the same meaning to an audience from other eras. With a Norman or French patron and Saxon artisans, the tapestry became a device in which to include subversive images while supporting the cause of the patrons. "It may also be seen as the work of a designer who did not see the issue in quite such black and white terms as his patron."[19] In many ways, the tapestry became both a Norman *and* Saxon source of the battle, but the tapestry can only provide its images as a skeleton of the story. Written text has provided the story of Hastings with flesh.

The historiography of Hastings has many sides. The Saxon chroniclers found fault in defeat with the sins of the people and the supposed perjury of Harold's oath of fealty to William. In truth, it is easy now to see fault with the unclear succession plans laid forth by Edward; however, in the eleventh century no fault was to be found in Edward. Those who fought alongside William or benefitted from the Conquest elevated William to the status of a liberator and savior of the English from the tyranny and oppression of the usurper Harold. The following generations were able to write more honestly about those involved, yet even then blood and position stood in the way of objective reporting. The heroic spirit of the Normans demanded that songs of lineage and great deeds be sung to honor those at Hastings. Those of mixed blood skirted the fine line between open acceptance of Harold's right and abilities with the truth of William's successful policies in England, despite their brutality. The landscape had changed drastically. The history is in the eye of the beholder.

What was the world like in which the history of Hastings was written? A strongly religious atmosphere gripped the British Isles and monastic reform was prevalent. Those conquered searched for meaning in defeat and found it in the sins of its people and in Harold, the king who failed to protect them from the Norman oppressors. The conquerors found vindication and justification in what was felt to be rightfully theirs. For the Normans, England had been promised to them and the attempt to steal it from them served only as a minor bump on the road to London. William evolved from a derisive reputation as a Bastard to a laudatory reputation as the Conqueror. Those who served him desired to commemorate the occasion with a tapestry extolling the greatness of the conquest. The generations which followed, those of mixed blood, searched for a more honest history, yet the entanglements of politics and society often interfered. The world of the historians of Hastings was one of retrospective divine justification and retribution. The question of succession and rule had been decided on the field of battle by divine right. The world made sense and England was to be thankful for its Norman lords. While there were still gentlemen in England filled with contempt and hatred, the successive generations of mixed heritage and Anglicizing of the Norman lords softened the blow. The Battle of Hastings reshaped the landscape of Europe and shifted the influences of the British Isles away from Scandinavia and towards the European Continent. Those who wrote of this lived in a world of change and uncertainty. The historiography of Hastings, whether from the conquerors or from the conquered, found common voice in actions while arguing the motives, oaths, and heirs of a dying culture and kingdom. The Saxon world had ended, replaced by a Norman one – but the conquered Saxons never quite disappeared.

Notes
    [1] Rev. James Ingram, trans., *The Anglo-Saxon Chronicle* (London: Everyman Press, 1912), 119.
    [2] Marjorie Chibnall, *The Debate on the Norman Conquest* (Manchester, UK: Manchester Press, 1999), 12.
    [3] Ibid, 121.
    [4] Ibid.
    [5] Marjorie Chibnall, *The World of Orderic Vitalis: Norman Monks and Knights* (Woodbridge, UK: The Boydell Press, 1996), 175.
    [6] Chibnall, *The Debate on the Norman Conquest*, 12.
    [7] Wace, *Roman de Rou*, trans. Edgar Taylor (London: William Pickering, 1837), 87.
    [8] Wace, 89.
    [9] Chibnall, *The World of Orderic Vitalis*, 4.
    [10] William of Malmesbury, *Chronicle of the Kings of England*, trans. J.A Giles (London: H.G. Bohn, 1847), 250.
    [11] Ibid, 254.
    [12] William of Malmesbury, 252.
    [13] Ibid, 252.
    [14] Chibnall, *The World of Orderic Vitalis*, 204.

[15] Ernst Breisach, *Historiography: Ancient, Medieval, and Modern* (Chicago: University of Chicago Press, 2007), 114-115.

[16] Andrew Bridgeford, *1066: The Hidden History of the Bayeux Tapestry* (New York: Walker Books, 2005), 308.

[17] David Howarth, *1066: The Year of the Conquest* (New York: Barnes & Noble Books, 1993), 182.

[18] Benton Rain Patterson, *Harold and William: The Battle for England , A.D. 1064-1066* (New York: Cooper Square Press, 2001), xviii.

[19] Harriet Harvey Wood, *The Battle of Hastings: The Fall of Anglo-Saxon England* (London: Atlantic Books, 2008), 230.

Bibliography

Bridgeford, Andrew. *1066: The Hidden History of the Bayeux Tapestry*. New York: Walker Books, 2005.

Brisach, Ernst. *Historiography: Ancient, Medieval, and Modern*. Chicago: University of Chicago Press, 2007.

Chibnall, Marjorie. *The Debate on the Norman Conquest*. Manchester, UK: Manchester Press, 1999.

Chibnall, Marjorie. *The World of Orderic Vitalis*. Woodbridge, UK: The Boydell Press, 1996.

Howarth, David. *1066: The Year of the Conquest*. New York: Barnes & Noble Books, 1993.

Ingram, Rev. James, trans. *The Anglo-Saxon Chronicle*. London: Everyman Press, 1912.

Patterson, Benton Rain. *Harold and William: The Battle for England, A.D. 1064-1066*. New York: Cooper Square Press, 2001.

Wace. *Roman de Rou*. Translated by Edgar Taylor. London: William Pickering, 1837.

William of Malmesbury. *Chronicle of the Kings of England*. Translated by J.A Giles. London: H.G. Bohn, 1847

Wood, Harriet Harvey. *The Battle of Hastings: The Fall of Anglo-Saxon England*. London: Atlantic Books, 2008.

The Ranger Raid on St. Francis

Francis M. Hoeflinger

The Ranger's Raid on St. Francis (4 October 1759)

Was the raid on St. Francis a proper mission for a Ranger force and did it have a strategic impact on the French and Indian War? The Ranger raid executed against the Abenaki Indians village of St. Francis on 4 October 1759 was conducted against the backdrop of the French and Indian War's Mohawk Valley theater of operations. However, addressing the question of the Ranger utility in conducting the raid also raises several additional questions: Was the raid effective? Did Roger's comply with his orders? Was the raid more of a propaganda victory than a tactical or strategic one? This paper will answer these questions as well as the veracity of the reporting on both sides.

Background on the French and Indian War

The French and Indian War was the name of the conflict fought in North America as part of the global conflict known as the Seven Years' War. The war was fought along the frontier between the French and British North American colonies from modern-day Nova Scotia south towards Virginia and as far west as modern-day Detroit. The genesis for the war was the dispute over natural resources and boundaries between the competing kingdoms and their subjects in the New World. The French began fortifying the "lands upon the River Ohio"[1] at the same time that the British Royal Colony of Virginia claimed the land. In response to the French actions, Virginia's governor, Robert Dinwiddie, sent a militia Major by the name of

George Washington to carry messages to the French in an attempt to resolve the dispute diplomatically at the local level.

A series of diplomatic and military moves and counter-moves ensued, culminating in Lieutenant Colonel Washington ambushing a diplomatic party and killing an officer of the French Royal Army.[2] Washington had been in the process of reinforcing Britain's claim to the area by building a compound later called Fort Necessity.[3] To exasperate matters even further, there were very different descriptions of the events leading up to the death of the French officer Ensign de Jumonville and nine of his men. Washington reported "We killed Mr. *de Jumonville*, the commander of the Party, as also nine others; we wounded one, and made Twenty-one Prisoners."[4] When diplomatic documents were discovered, the true intent of the French patrol was realized.[5]

The French claimed that one of their soldiers escaped the initial ambush and watched as members of Washington's patrol murdered the ensign in cold blood.[6] To make matters worse for the British, Washington had placed his "fort" in an indefensible position and the French forced him to surrender. As part of the capitulation, Washington signed the surrender document (written in French), without (in his words) understanding what he was signing. What was included in the document was the statement that Washington had "murdered" Ensign de Jumonville. This led to active combat in the North American Theater.[7]

The fighting in the North American Theater pitted the French military and militia units and their Native American allies against the British forces and their Native American allies. The French attempted to maximize their combat power by enlisting the various tribes in the area to supply warriors to supplement French forces and to conduct independent operations in support of French military objectives.

The British felt that the addition of the Native American contingent to the French forces placed them at a disadvantage, and attempted to recruit Native American tribes to their cause. This caused difficulties for the various Native American Tribes that lived in the North American Theater of operations, because it pitted nominal Indian allies against each other. The contentious subject of religion added to the already grand animosity. The French were a predominantly Catholic nation and the British predominantly Protestant. Additionally, some of the individual Native American Tribes had converted to one of the European religious denominations. The Abenaki had converted to Catholicism in the 17th Century.[8]

The French and Indian War in New England

This article will concentrate on the Mohawk River Valley and the New England area of Operations of the French and Indian War. The year 1759 would prove pivotal for British fortunes in North America. The "de facto" British Prime Minister, William Pitt, was determined to make the year 1759 pivotal by defeating the French in North America before turning his attention to other theaters of operation.[9] The British strategy was to concentrate their force in actions along the eastern Great Lakes and the St. Lawrence River. The British succeeded in gaining victories at the battles of Fort Niagara (6 – 26 July 1759),[10] La Belle-Famille (24 July 1759),[11] Fort Carillion (26 -27 July 1759),[12] and the Plains of Abraham (13 September 1759).[13] The Battle for Fort William Henry was a disastrous defeat for the British, because of the massacre of the garrison and their family members by the Abenaki Indians who were aligned with the French after the French accepted the garrison's surrender and agreed to let them leave under a flag of truce.[14]

General Jeffrey Amherst then decided to launch a raid against the Abenaki base of operations, the village of St. Francis. The Abenaki had been raiding and pillaging the English settlements along the Atlantic coast in modern New England since at least the seventeenth century. Amherst also desired to destroy the myth of Indian invulnerability in "woodland" fighting.

Major Robert Rogers

Major Robert Rogers was probably the most famous "woodland" fighter of his day. Rogers was born around 1731 in the colony of Massachusetts Bay and spent his formative years in the New Hampshire back-country. Rogers spent his early youth hunting and exploring the woods.[15] Rogers first encountered and became fascinated with the American Indians in his youth, studying their ways, culture, habits and even language.[16] Rogers first gained combat experience when he joined the Militia Company from Rumford Massachusetts in 1746, and fought Indian raiders until the end of the King George's War in 1748.[17]

Rogers earned a commission from Governor Shirley, when he raised enough recruits for the French and Indian War, and became the unit's Captain. Rogers' utility to the British became critical through a series of scouting missions and long distance raids that he and his men successfully conducted. Authorized by Amherst to raise a "Regiment of Rangers," Rogers succeeded in drawing high quality recruits to his unit.

Overview of the conduct of the raid 4 October 1759

Rogers left with two hundred handpicked Rangers and proceeded by boat up Lake Champlain. Rogers left a security element at the site chosen to cache the boats and proceeded overland towards his target. French soldiers on patrol discovered Rogers' cache site, and the security element caught up with Rogers and warned him of the loss.[18] The loss of the cache site was a twofold problem for Rogers. He not only lost the planned mode of transportation back to Crown Point, he also lost all the provisions stored at the cache site to sustain the Rangers after the raid during the exfiltration.

The Abenaki, forewarned that there was enemy (British) activity in the area, moved the majority of their warriors to the village they believed to be Rogers' actual target. The Ranger leaders, as would be recognizable by any modern Infantryman, conducted a reconnaissance of the village and determined the village layout, including the location of the key buildings, the communal storehouse and the Catholic Church. The Rangers set a cordon on the far side of the village along the St. Francis river, a probable escape route, and were ordered to kill any Indians that attempted to escape in that direction. Rogers' plan was to divide his force into three elements. Each element would attack a different sector of the village. Rogers detailed the Rangers either to attack a specific building, or to act as sharpshooters, engaging any combatant when possible.[19] Rogers attacked at 0515hrs[20] and claimed that the Abenaki were unable to offer effective resistance and the raid was over by 0700hrs. Rogers looted the community storehouse and burned the entire village, including the church, to the ground.

Controversy surrounding Abenaki casualties

Rogers took almost six weeks to travel from his base camp at Crown Point to the Village of St. Francis, approximately one hundred fifty miles north of Crown Point. After the raid, he and his men evaded capture and returned to Fort Number 4 in modern-day

Connecticut. Rogers claimed that he lost three officers and forty-six men out of a force of one hundred forty-two Rangers that conducted the raid.[21] Rogers claimed that he incurred the majority of his casualties during the French pursuit of his force back to Fort Number 4. Rogers claimed that only one Ranger had been killed during the raid and seven Rangers were wounded. According to Rogers' report of the action, sixty-five to one hundred forty warriors were killed, twenty Indian women and children were captured and later released, five English prisoners were liberated, and Chief Gill's wife, two sons and three daughters were captured. This seems to be an unexplainably small number of casualties compared to the number of Indians he claimed to have been killed or captured. Additionally, the Rangers captured enough corn to sustain them for the first eight days of their escape and evasion back to English territory.

The Abenaki claim to have put up stout resistance and to have killed forty Rangers. The Abenaki claim cannot be discounted at face value. The Rangers had lost the strategic element of surprise due to the discovery of their boats at the cache site. According to Abenaki oral history, an unnamed warrior came to the Village of St. Francis the night before the raid to warn the village that the British were nearby.[22] The Abenaki claimed that they had moved the majority of their women, children, and elderly members to another village,[23] and that only warriors remained to defend the village. This would explain their stout defense and claims of significant Ranger casualties. Which side has left the most credible history? It is impossible based on the historical evidence to say definitively which version of events is the most accurate. It is unusual for both sides to agree, independently of each other, on the number of Ranger casualties (to re-state, the Abenaki claim they inflicted forty casualties, and Rogers admits to forty-nine total casualties). While the numbers do not match exactly, it is highly improbable that they would be so close coincidentally. It is probable that the Abenaki did inflict the number of casualties claimed and that Rogers lost the additional nine Rangers during the escape and evasion back to Fort Number 4.

Aftermath of the raid

The survivors of the raid were then forced to escape and evade across country in an unplanned direction because of the discovery and destruction of their boats and all the provision stored there. The evasion started well but became a survival trek. The food ran out after eight days, and the French and Abenaki organized patrols to hunt for and ambush any Rangers they could find. "Major Rogers, upon receiving the news of the French and Indian force in pursuit, dispatch Lt. McMullen to return to Crown Point. His mission was to prepare of reception party for the Rangers."[24] The Rangers eventually decided that it would be better to break up into smaller units and attempt to evade their way, independent of each other, to Fort Number 4.[25] Some units became so famished that the capture of a "red squirrel was an event."[26] Many years after the fact, a member of the Royal Army attached to the Rangers reported that the men resorted to cannibalism to survive their harrowing ordeal.[27] It is impossible, both because of the paucity of detailed records and the hectic and harrowing ordeal, to determine exactly how many Rangers were captured and killed by the French or Abenaki patrols. Major Rogers, after organizing search and rescue parties, to guide his dispersed Ranger force back to friendly lines, composed his report and sent it off to General Amherst. The raid, based solely on Rogers' report, was declared an unheralded success, and immediately had an effect on the morale of the military and civilian populations of British North America. The raid and its aftermath were trumpeted in newspapers in New York City.[28] No longer could the Native

American tribes aligned with the French conduct operations against British military or civilian targets with impunity.[29] The Native Americans would now have to contend with the possibility that Rogers' Corps of Rangers would conduct an attack against their villages when the warriors were away on a mission.

What was the strategic effect, if any, of the raid on the conduct of the war in New England?

What was achieved by the loss of highly skilled, well trained and battle hardened Rangers? The propaganda value of the raid was incalculable, but wars are not won by the weight of a single propaganda victory regardless of its size. Rogers claimed to have killed two hundred Abenaki warriors, destroyed their village, and dispersed the surviving women and children. If so, the raid would be a blow from which the Abenaki would not quickly recover.

There is no historical evidence to indicate that the Abenaki Indians ever waivered in their support of the French until the French were finally defeated and the French colony transferred to British control. After the war, the Abenaki migrated back to their traditional hunting grounds and persevered.

Finally, was the raid a mission within the capabilities and limitations of the Ranger Regiment as it was trained and organized in 1759? Unequivocally, the answer is yes. The Rangers traveled over one hundred fifty miles from their base at Crown Point to their target of the Village of St. Francis, on the St. Francis River, just south of the Saint Lawrence River. The Rangers conducted the infiltration and raid as planned. In accordance with Rogers' command philosophy, a fragmentary order was issued to change the exfiltration from a riverine movement to an overland exfiltration. It was decided to re-supply from the community stores at the target. This major change of plan could have only been executed, already far behind enemy lines, by a well-trained and confident force.

The raid on St. Francis was a proper mission for a Ranger force and it had strategic impact on the French and Indian War, albeit largely as a propaganda victory. The Rangers executed the raid against the Abenaki Indians Village of St. Francis on 4 October 1759 and conducted it against the background of the French and Indian War's Mohawk Valley theater of operations. The Raid was a propaganda victory, but did not contribute materially to the war effort.

Notes

[1] Fred Anderson, *Crucible of War: The Seven Years War and the Fate of Empire in British North America, 1754 – 1766* (New York: Vintage Books, 2000), 44.

[2] Anderson, *Crucible*, 55.

[3] Ibid., 52.

[4] Ibid., 53.

[5] Ibid.

[6] Ibid., 54.

[7] Ibid., 64.

[8] Frank McLynn, *1759: The Year Britain Became Master of the World* (New York: Grove Press, 2004), 332.

[9] McLynn, *1759*, 95.

[10] McLynn, *1759*, 149-152.

[11] Anderson, *Crucible of War*, 337.

[12] McLynn, *1759*, 154-155.

[13] McLynn, *1759*, 300-309.

[14] Anderson, *Crucible of War*, 197.

[15] John F. Ross, *War on the Run, The Epic Story of Robert Rogers and the Conquest of America's First Frontier* (New York: Bantam Books, 2009), 20.

[16] Ibid., 26-27.

[17] Ibid., 43-44.

[18] Burt G. Loescher, *The History of Rogers' Rangers, Vol. 2: Genesis, the First Green Berets, April 6, 1758 – December 24, 1783.* 1969. (Bowie, MD: Heritage, 2000), 58.

[19] Ross, *War on the Run*, 250.

[20] Burt G. Loescher, *The History of Rogers' Rangers, Vol. IV: The St. Francis Raid*, 1969. Westminster, Heritage Books, 2008, 38.

[21] Ibid., 268.

[22] Deborah P. Clifford, "The Raid On St. Francis," *Historic Roots*, no. 3 (December 1997): 19-20.

[23] Loescher, *The History of Rogers' Rangers, Vol. IV*, 38.

[24] MSG Walter H. Sargent, *The Emergence of the American Noncommissioned Officer: Rogers' Rangers During the French and Indian War from 1754 to 1763*, Combined Arms Research Library, United States Army Sergeants Major Academy Collection, 8.

[25] Ross, *War on the Run*, 258.

[26] Colonel Red Reeder, *The French and Indian War*, Kindle Edition, (Quechee, Vermont Heritage Press, 2011), position 1713 of 2517.

[27] Ian McCulloch, Tim J. Todish, *British Light Infantryman of the Seven Years' War: North America 1757 – 63* (Oxford: Osprey Publishing, 2004), 28.

[28] Ross, *War on the Run*, 268.

[29] Ibid., 269-270.

Bibliography

Anderson, Fred. *Crucible of War: The Seven Years War and the Fate of Empire in British North America, 1754 – 1766*. New York: Vintage Books, 2000.

Clifford, Deborah P. "The Raid On St. Francis." *Historic Roots*, No 3, December 1997, pg. 17-22.

Loescher, Burt G. *The History of Rogers' Rangers, Vol. 2: Genesis, the First Green Berets, April 6, 1758 – December 24, 1783*. 1969. Bowie, MD: Heritage, 2000.

—. *The History of Rogers' Rangers, Vol. IV: The St. Francis Raid*, 1969. Westminster, Heritage Books, 2008.

McCulloch, Ian and Tim J. Todish. *British Light Infantryman of the Seven Years' War: North America 1757 – 63*. Oxford: Osprey Publishing, 2004.

McLynn, Frank. *1759: The Year Britain Became Master of the World*. New York: Grove Press, 2004.

Reeder, Colonel Red. *The French and Indian War*. Quechee, Vermont Heritage Press, 2011. Kindle.

Ross, John F. *War on the Run, The Epic Story of Robert Rogers and the Conquest of America's First Frontier*. New York: Bantam Books, 2009.

Sargent, MSG Walter H. *The Emergence of the American Noncommissioned Officer: Rogers' Rangers During the French and Indian War from 1754 to 1763*. Combined Arms Research Library, United States Army Sergeants Major Academy Collection.

U. S. Air Force Medals of Honor
Justin Brian McDonald

The United States Air Force is the newest branch of the United States military. Since its inception in 1947, the Air Force has had eighteen Medal of Honor recipients.[1] These recipients differ from those in the Army, Marines, Navy and Coast Guard in the scope of their mission and objectives but not in their courage, bravery, and commitment to honor and discipline in fighting.

To understand the significance of the Air Force Medal of Honor recipients, it is essential to understand the importance of the Air Force as a whole and where its specific mission originated. Throughout the twentieth century, the Army had been utilizing the idea of aircraft, from the simple balloon for observation to planes for precision bombing and close air support. Early in World War One, the idea of aircraft expanding and improving the battle-space began.

During the interwar period between the end of World War One and the onset of World War Two, military and civilian philosophers around the world created new ideas on the tactics of war. These interwar tank prophets included John Frederick Charles (J.F.C.) Fuller (1878-1966), Basil Henry (B.H.) Liddell Hart (1895-1970), and, arguably, Adolph Hitler.[2] The devastation caused by trench warfare in World War One spread worldwide, and philosophers were looking for a way to improve the mobility of maneuver warfare via land or air.

The importance of tank warfare was shown partially in World War One and expanded during the interwar period. Others, however, believed that the true key to unlocking mobility was in aerial warfare. During the interwar period, philosophers like Italian General

Giulio Douhet (1869-1930) advocated for an increase in airpower. He believed that strategic bombing paved the way for eliminating stagnant trench warfare.[3] This led to his work *The Command of the Air,* published in 1921, a piece that was considered the first detailed analysis of the offensive and defensive employment of aircraft. In *The Command of the Air* he first presented his "four basic truths" which all revolved around the evolution of warfare and its uses in the future.[4]

Douhet was a contemporary to the man who is largely considered the father of the United States Air Force, United States Army Brigadier General William "Billy" Mitchell (1879-1936). Mitchell served in France toward the end of World War One and commanded all American air combat units. After World War One, he was appointed deputy director of Air Service. Mitchell was so adamant about the use of air power that he was demoted from brigadier general to colonel in 1925 because of his outspoken criticism of the Army's use, or lack of use, of air power. Later in the same year, he was court-martialed for accusing Army and Navy leaders of "incompetency, criminal negligence, and almost treasonable administration of the National Defense" for investing in battleships instead of carriers to further development of air forces.[5]

Mitchell was able to show in live fire demonstrations on 21 July 1921 that his air forces were effective both on land and at sea. The United States purchased the ex-German World War One battleship *Ostfriesland* and used it for Mitchell's demonstration. He substantiated his claims that air forces were superior to naval forces (much to the disdain of upper leadership in government and civilian components) when his air forces sank the *Ostfriesland* in twenty-one and a half minutes with aerial bombardment.[6]

It was not until the United States entered World War Two and saw the value of close air support and strategic bombing in breaking down trench warfare that Mitchell's ideas were condoned by upper leadership in the United States government. It was not until eleven years after his death, on 18 September 1947, that the United States Air Force was formed. Stuart Symington became the first Secretary of the Air Force and General Carl A. Spaatz became the first Chief of Staff. On 14 October 1947, not even a month after the inception of the Air Force, Chuck Yeager conducted his infamous flight that thrust the Bell XS-1 past the speed of sound, an event that ushered the Air Force into the supersonic era.[7]

The Air Force has participated in limited conflicts since its inception due to its different mission from any other branch of the military. The missions of the Army, Marines, or Navy cannot offer the distinctive opportunities that members of the Air Force have, such as aerial supply, logistics, fighting and bombing. The Air Force has produced eighteen Medal of Honor recipients. Of these eighteen, fourteen men from the Vietnam War and four from the Korean War were awarded. Unlike other branches, officers comprised a high percentage of recipients for the Air Force because they make up a large part of the crew of aircraft. Only three out of eighteen recipients have been enlisted members.[8]

The first major conflict in which the fledgling Air Force participated was the Korean War (1950-1953). During this conflict, 131 Medals of Honor were awarded to U.S. servicemen, four of those from the Air Force. Since the Air Force had not yet designed its own version of the Medal, they were awarded the Army version of the Medal of Honor.[9]

Aside from the history of the Air Force, it is also important to understand the background and requirements for the nation's highest military award, the Medal of Honor. Former Air Force Chief of Staff John D. Ryan described the requirements as, "A member of the American Armed Forces can merit the Medal of Honor in only one manner: by a deed of personal bravery or self-sacrifice, above and beyond the call of duty, while in combat with an enemy of the nation. The gallantry must be certified by two eye-witnesses, and be clearly beyond the call of duty. Moreover, it must involve the risk of life and must be the type of deed that, if not performed, would evoke no criticism of the individual."[10]

The first recipient from the Air Force was Major Louis J. Sebille. On 5 August 1950, Sebille was commanding the 67th Fighter-Bomber Squadron. On a mission that night he led a flight of F-51 Mustangs against a communist artillery and troop position for a bombing run on the banks of a river near Hamchang, South Korea. One of Sebille's 500-pound bombs stuck during his first pass and would not release. This caused instability in the aircraft and an immediate request for him to break away and return to base. Despite this request, Sebille came in for a second pass, firing his machine guns on the enemy position. He then made a third pass, during which his aircraft was mortally damaged. Sebille, realizing the extent of the damage, deliberately flew his aircraft into the communist positions. On 24 August 1951, Air Force Chief of Staff General Hoyt S. Vandenberg presented the Medal of Honor to Sebille's widow.[11]

Captain John S. Walmsley, Jr. showed exemplary courage while utilizing a piece of test equipment, a spotlight mounted on aircraft to target enemy positions. During his tests on 14 September 1951, his aircraft was severely damaged, yet he continued to make additional passes on an enemy train to illuminate the way for other aircraft to attack. He was awarded the Medal of Honor on 12 June 1954.[12]

At the time of his death, Major George A. Davis, Jr. was the leading American ace of the Korean War, with 11 MiG-15 and three Tu-2 bomber kills to his credit. On 10 February 1952, he scored two of those kills against a group of roughly a dozen enemy MiG-15s.

His actions on that day saved a squadron of fighter-bombers attacking targets near the Yalu River. He was awarded the Medal of Honor on 14 May 1952.[13]

Major Charles J. Loring, Jr., in a deliberate and controlled maneuver, dove his severely damaged aircraft into a group of active enemy gun emplacements on 22 November 1952. He was awarded the Medal of Honor on 5 May 1954. All four Air Force Medal of Honor recipients from the Korean War were awarded posthumously. All four were officers.[14]

After the Korean War ended in 1953, the next major conflict in which the United States Air Force would see action was the Vietnam War. There have been 248 medals of Honor received for actions during this war. Of these, 156 were presented posthumously. Only fourteen were presented to members of the Air Force. Until 8 December 2000, this number was only twelve. On that date, Airman First Class William H. Pitsenbarger's Air Force Cross was upgraded to a Medal of Honor. In 2010, Chief Master Sergeant Richard L. Etchberger's Air Force Cross was also upgraded after his mission was finally declassified. This brought the number to fourteen for the Air Force.[15]

The Air Force finally adopted its own version of the Medal of Honor in 1965. Major Bernard F. Fisher was the first to receive this version, the first Airman in Vietnam to receive the award, and the first living Air Force member to receive the Medal of Honor.[16]

On 10 March 1966, Fisher flew in a four-aircraft formation composed of A-1Es, that was part of a bombing run in support of American and South Vietnamese troops pinned down in the A Shau Valley. On their second pass, one of Fisher's wingmen, Captain Hubert King, was hit and forced to land his crumbling plane in the middle of the attacking North Vietnamese. With helicopters more than twenty minutes out and the North Vietnamese closing quickly on King's position, Fisher landed his aircraft in an attempt to save King. He made a spectacular landing, and King was able to make his way to the aircraft. They both escaped with their lives and Fisher was awarded with not only the Medal of Honor, but his wingman's immense gratitude.[17]

During a rescue mission on 1 September 1968, another A-1 pilot, Colonel William A. Jones III, flew extremely low in order to locate a downed F-100 fighter, call-sign Carter 02 Alpha. When initial passes did not reveal the exact location, Jones flew deep into the valley, exposing himself to intense enemy fire. Almost immediately upon locating the downed aircraft, Jones's plane burst into flames around the cockpit. His communications were destroyed, his ejection mechanism did not function properly, his canopy had ejected, and flames were licking his face and hands. Suffering from severe burns to his hands, arms, shoulders, neck, and face, Colonel Jones still piloted his aircraft ninety miles, for over forty minutes of flying time, back to base. He landed the aircraft with help from his wingman and refused medical attention until he could point out exactly where Carter 02 Alpha was located and the position of the surrounding enemy guns.[18]

Also presented the Medal of Honor during the Vietnam War were two Forward Air Controllers, Captain Hilliard A. Wilbanks and Captain Steven L. Bennett; two members of the infamous Wild Weasels, Major Merlyn H. Dethlefsen and Major Leo K. Thorsness; two helicopter pilots, Captain Gerald O. Young and First Lieutenant James P. Fleming; and a C-123 pilot Lieutenant Joe Jackson who made a heroic rescue landing in his cargo plane on a check flight, Mother's Day, 1968.[19]

The first enlisted man to earn the Air Force Medal of Honor was John L. Levitow, an airman first class, or E-3. This was the third lowest rank possible in the United States Air Force, and his duties were supposed to be simple and monotonous. Levitow was attached to the 3rd Special Operations Squadron that flew the AC-47 (predecessor to today's AC130 "Spooky" gunships). On 24 February 1969, Levitow stepped in for the normal loadmaster on "Spooky 71." As they took off for their normal mission that night in the Tan Son Nhut Air Base area, the U.S. Army base at Long Binh came under heavy attack. "Spooky 71" was dispatched and fired thousands of rounds at the enemy troops in support of U.S. ground troops.[20]

The other major mission of the modified C-47's was to drop M-24 magnesium flares out of the open cargo hatch in order to illuminate the battlefield. Levitow was on his 180th combat mission. His responsibility that night was to remove the flares from a safety rack, set the controls and pass them to the gunner who would pull the pin and throw them out of the cargo door. The fuse was set on these flares for twenty seconds before they would ignite. Once ignited, they would burn at over 4,000 degrees Fahrenheit.[21]

During the fifth hour of support, a Viet Cong 82mm mortar shell clipped the right wing of "Spooky 71" and exploded. This blew a two foot in diameter hole in the hull and spread shrapnel throughout the aircraft. Forty pieces of shrapnel hit Levitow in his back and legs. All four other crewmen in the cargo area were wounded as well. The gunner had just pulled the safety pin out of a magnesium flare and was preparing to throw it out when the plane was struck and he was hit with shrapnel, which caused him to drop the flare in the plane's cargo bay.[22]

As Levitow was already moving wounded crewmen away from the door he noticed the flare rolling around inside the bay. He knew that if the flare ignited, it would set off the thousands of rounds of ammunition that were still on the aircraft. As Levitow desperately tried to grasp the flare, with the plane in a sharp banked turn, he realized that he could not just pick it up. He threw himself on the flare to stop it from rolling around. He then dragged it to the cargo door, leaving a trail of blood as he limped, partially paralyzed from the shrapnel in his back, towards the opening. He hurled the flare out of the rear cargo door right as it ignited.[23]

Once the plane landed safely at Bien Hoa, the damage to the aircraft became evident. "Spooky 71" had more than 3500 holes in the wings and fuselage, including one more than three feet long. Levitow was sent to Tachikawa, Japan and spent two months recovering from his wounds. He then returned to Vietnam for combat but was grounded on his third mission because his chain-of-command informed him that he had been nominated for the Medal of Honor.[24]

Two Medals of Honor were awarded to Air Force members who were Prisoners of War (POW) during Vietnam. The first was Major George E. Day, a POW from 26 August 1967 until 14 March 1973. Harshly tortured, Day refused to divulge any information that could harm his fellow prisoners or the airmen who still operated against the enemy. He even managed to escape for twelve days before being recaptured. He held true to the Code of Conduct of military personnel and represented his country with honor as a POW. He was released with his fellow prisoners after five and a half years of captivity.[25]

Captain Lance P. Sijan was the other POW who received the Medal of Honor for his actions. After being shot down, Sijan ejected and drifted into a heavily forested area. He was knocked unconscious as he landed roughly in the thick trees. On 10 November 1967, Sijan regained consciousness and realized the extent of his injuries. He had suffered a compound fracture of his left leg, a crushed right hand, several head injuries, and several deep lacerations.[26]

Despite these injuries, Sijan was able to evade capture for forty-five days. Once imprisoned, he held stringently to the Code of Conduct and refused to give any information, other than that required by Article V: "When questioned, should I become a prisoner of war, I am required to give name, rank, service number, and date of birth. I will evade answering further questions to the utmost of my ability. I will make no oral or written statements disloyal to my country and its allies or harmful to their cause."[27]

He escaped briefly and continued to attempt to escape for the duration of his capture. When his injuries were so bad that he could not support his own body weight, Sijan requested that his cell mates prop him up against his bed so he could exercise his arms in preparation for yet another breakout. Sijan died in captivity in the Hanoi Hilton on 22 January 1968. On 4 March 1976, Sijan became the first, and at that time, the only graduate of the United States Air Force Academy to be awarded the Medal of Honor.[28]

This rounded out the twelve recipients who were originally awarded the Medal of Honor during the Vietnam War. On 8 December 2000, Airman First Class William H. Pitsenbarger became the second enlisted man to receive the award. On this date, his Air Force Cross was upgraded to the Medal of Honor. Pitsenbarger was assigned to the 38th Air Rescue and Recovery Squadron at Bien Hoa Air Base near Saigon. On 11 April 1966, Pitsenbarger and his team were dispatched to extract several Army casualties from a unit near the village of Cam My, a few miles east of Saigon.[29]

Pitsenbarger was lowered with the hoist to assist in loading casualties. After the first extraction, he chose to stay on the ground with the wounded. During the second attempted extraction, the helicopters came under fire and were hit. Pitsenbarger chose to remain on the ground yet again. He helped hold off the enemy but was killed during the night by Viet Cong snipers. When his body was recovered the next day, one hand still clutched his rifle and the other his medical aid kit that he had been using to tend the wounded while fighting the enemy. On 22 September 1966, he became the first enlisted man to receive the Air Force Cross posthumously. It was upgraded to the Medal of Honor thirty-four years later.[30]

The final recipient was Chief Master Sergeant (CMSgt) Richard L. Etchberger. The actions that merited his Medal of Honor were performed on 10 March 1968, but Etchberger's mission was so highly classified, the award could not be considered at the time. While working at a radar site in Laos, the site came under attack. Etchberger selflessly fought off the enemy with his M-16 while trying to save his comrades. Out of the original nineteen Americans at the site, only Etchberger and six others survived when the rescue helicopter arrived. He helped load the wounded onto slings and was the last off the rooftop. As the helicopter was flying away, enemy AK-47 rounds burst through the underside of the helicopter, killing Etchberger.[31]

John Daniels was one of the survivors. He had been shot twice when Etchberger found him and helped him into the litter to be evacuated. At the Medal of Honor ceremony for Etchberger in 2010, Daniels said, "He should have a 55-gallon drum full of medals. I wouldn't be alive without him. Forty-two plus years too goddamn late. It should have happened forty-two plus years ago."[32]

Along with their fellow awardees from the Army, Marines, Navy and Coast Guard, these eighteen recipients have become role models for all branches of the American military. Their commitment to the United States, its Code of Conduct, and their fellow airmen showed an exemplary level of dedication that other airmen can only hope to replicate.

During a Medal of Honor presentation ceremony at the White House, President Harry S. Truman said, "I would rather have this medal than be President of the United States." The "medals of honor" were created in 1862, when President Abraham Lincoln approved an Act of Congress authorizing them. A single word is etched on each of these medals to tell their meaning. That word is simple, yet defines the character of each of the eighteen United States Air Force recipients discussed above. Even though the Air Force is the youngest of the services, a mere child compared to the other branches, receiving the Medal of Honor merits just as much credit. They wear the Medal of Honor with honor and pride for their country, freedom, and the brothers and sisters who have come before and will come after them. The word etched on the face of every Medal of Honor defines their actions. That word? VALOR.[33]

Notes

[1] "United States Air Force Medal of Honor Recipients," Congressional Medal of Honor Society, http://www.cmohs.org/search-results.php?q=&rank=&organization=U.S. Air Force&division=&company=&conflict=&x=62&y=12 (accessed March 17, 2014).

[2] Brian Holden Reid, "J.F.C. Fuller: From Practice to Theory" *History Today* 39, no. 6 (June 1989), 44.

[3] Michael J. Eula, "Giulio Douhet and Strategic Air Force Operations," *Air University Review,* (September/October 1986), 95.

[4] John F. Shiner, "Reflections on Douhet: The Classic Approach," *Air University Review,* (January/February, 1986), 94.

[5] William Mitchell, *William "Billy" Mitchell's Airpower,* Compiled by Johnny R. Jones for the Air University. Air Power Research Institute, Maxwell Air Force Base, 1997, xi-xiv.

[6] Ibid., xiii.

[7] "Air Power Comes of Age in World War II," AirForce.Com, http://www.airforce.com/learn-about/history/part2/ (accessed March 17, 2014).

[8] "United States Air Force Medal of Honor Recipients," Congressional Medal of Honor Society, http://www.cmohs.org/search-results.php?q=&rank=&organization=U.S. Air Force&division=&company=&conflict=&x=62&y=12 (accessed March 17, 2014).

[9] Tom Yblood, "US Air Force Korean War Medal of Honor Recipients," Office of the Air Force Historian, http://www.nj.gov/military/korea/factsheets/medals.html (accessed March 17, 2014).

[10] Donald Schneider, "Air Force Heroes in Vietnam," *USAF Southeast Asia Monograph* 8 (1979), http://www.afhso.af.mil/shared/media/document/AFD-101004-030.pdf (accessed March 17, 2014), v.

[11] Yblood.

[12] Ibid.

[13] Ibid.

[14] Ibid.

[15] James H. Willbanks, ed., *America's Heroes: Medal of Honor Recipients from the Civil War to Afghanistan* (Santa Barbara, California.: ABC-CLIO, LLC, 2011), 261-63.

[16] Ibid.

[17] Schneider, 3-8.

[18] Ibid., 8-11.

[19] Ibid., 13-51.

[20] "Airman 1st Class John L. Levitow," Air Mobility Command Museum, http://amcmuseum.org/history/medal_of_honor/a1c_levitow.php (accessed March 17, 2014).

[21] Willbanks, 180-82.

[22] Ibid., 180-82.

[23] Ibid., 180-82.

[24] Ibid., 182.

[25] Schneider, 57-59.

[26] John L. Frisbee, "Valor: Lance Sijan's Incredible Journey," *Air Force Magazine* 69 (1986), 116. http://www.airforcemag.com/MagazineArchive/Documents/1986/December 1986/1286valor.pdf (accessed March 17, 2014).

[27] Robert K. Ruhl, "The Code of Conduct," AirForce.Mil, http://www.au.af.mil/au/awc/awcgate/au-24/ruhl.pdf (accessed March 17, 2014).

[28] Frisbee, 116.

[29] Willbanks, 261-62.

[30] Ibid., 262-63.

[31] John T. Correll, "Etchberger, Medal of Honor," *Air Force Magazine; vol.* 93, no. 11. (November 2010), 1.

[32] Ibid.

[33] Schneider, v-vii.

Bibliography

"Airman 1st Clast John L Levitow." Air Mobility Command Museum. http://amcmuseum.org/history/medal_of_honor/a1c_levitow.php (accessed March 17, 2014).

"Air Power Comes of Age in World War II." AirForce.Com. http://www.airforce.com/learn-about/history/part2/ (accessed March 17, 2014).

Correll, John T. "Etchberger, Medal of Honor." *Air Force Magazine;* 93, no. 11, (November 2010), 1. http://www.airforcemag.com/MagazineArchive/Pages/2010/November%202010/1110MOH.aspx (accessed March 17, 2014).

Eula, Michael J. "Giulio Douhet and Strategic Air Force Operations." *Air University Review.* (September/October 1986), 94-99.

Frisbee, John L. "Valor: Lance Sijan's Incredible Journey." *Air Force Magazine* 69 (December 1986), 116. http://www.airforcemag.com/MagazineArchive/Documents/1986/December 1986/1286valor.pdf (accessed March 17, 2014).

"Medal of Honor Recipients: Korea." Center of Military History. http://www.history.army.mil/moh/koreanwar.html (accessed March 17, 2014).

"Medal of Honor Recipients: Vietnam A-L." Center of Military History. http://www.history.army.mil/moh/vietnam-a-l.html (accessed March 17, 2014).

"Medal of Honor Recipients: Vietnam M-Z." Center of Military History. http://www.history.army.mil/moh/vietnam-m-z.html (accessed March 17, 2014).

Mitchell, William. *William "Billy" Mitchell's Airpower.* Compiled by Johnny R. Jones for the Air University. Air Power Research Institute. Maxwell Air Force Base, 1997.

Reid, Brian Holden. "J.F.C. Fuller: From Practice to Theory" *History Today* Vol. 39, Issue 6, June 1989, 44-50.

Ruhl, Robert K. "The Code of Conduct." AirForce.Mil. http://www.au.af.mil/au/awc/awcgate/au-24/ruhl.pdf (accessed March 17, 2014).

Schneider, Donald. "Air Force Heroes in Vietnam." *USAF Southeast Asia Monograph* 8 (1979), http://www.afhso.af.mil/shared/media/document/AFD-101004-030.pdf (accessed March 17, 2014).

Shiner, John F. "Reflections on Douhet: The Classic Approach" *Air University Review.* (January/February, 1986), 93-95.

"United States Air Force Medal of Honor Recipients." Congressional Medal of Honor Society. http://www.cmohs.org/search-results.php?q=&rank=&organization=U.S. Air Force&division=&company=&conflict=&x=62&y=12 (accessed March 17, 2014).

Willbanks, James H. ed. *America's Heroes: Medal of Honor Recipients from the Civil War to Afghanistan.* Santa Barbara, California: ABC-CLIO, LLC, 2011.

Yblood, Tom. "US Air Force Korean War Medal of Honor Recipients." Office of the Air Force Historian. http://www.nj.gov/military/korea/factsheets/medals.html (accessed March 17, 2014).

Students of War: Books and the Education of the American Continental Army

Anne Midgley

General George Washington, the commander-in-chief of the American Continental Army, may not have had an advanced education according to the customs of his day but he placed great value on the benefits that Continental Army officers could gain from a broad-based study of military texts. In a large degree due to his influence and exhortations, military books supplemented the hard lessons learned on the battlefield and shaped the development of many Continental Army officers. Studying classical military history and many other categories of military texts was not a unique practice of the American Patriots, but had been adopted from the example of British Army officers who had long relied on military treatises to prepare officers for their roles in the army and continue their education.

While they initially undertook their military studies before acquaintance with Washington, self-taught men like Henry Knox and Nathanael Greene who had no previous military experience became competent commanders in part due to their studies of military texts. Knox and Greene rapidly gained Washington's respect and became two of his most capable and trusted subordinates; they exemplified the value of military study to supplement innate leadership skills. Washington was known to exhort his officers to put aside gaming and instead devote their free time to study. He noted in his General Orders of 8 May 1777 that nothing "would redound more to their honor...than to devote the vacant moments...to the study of Military authors."[1]

After the outbreak of war with the French and their Native American allies in 1754, Washington, who had led Virginia's provincial troops in the earliest stages of the French and Indian War, began to supplement his practical experience with military studies. As early as 1755, he ordered *A Treatise of Military Discipline* by Humphrey Bland. Washington was influenced by the British officers whom he admired and sought to emulate; he adopted their practice of reading military texts. He had likely learned of Bland's book from British Commander-in-Chief Major General Edward Braddock. Washington had joined Braddock's army without pay, serving in a junior capacity in the hope that he could win a British officer's commission. He served as Braddock's aide-de-camp during the ill-fated British campaign to the Monongahela in 1754, which resulted in Braddock's death.[2] Washington's military education advanced rapidly in the fires of war, but he also benefitted from the reading recommendations of more senior officers. For instance, in 1756, Colonel William Fairfax, one of Washington's earliest mentors, wrote to Washington, "I am sensible that such a medley of undisciplined militia must create you various troubles, but, having Caesar's Commentaries, and perhaps Quintus Curtius, you have therein read of greater fatigues."[3]

Washington was not alone in adopting the study of military literature from the example of the British Army officers. For those in the Continental Army of the American War for Independence, studying military histories and technical treatises supplemented the meager experience they had relative to their foes in the British Army.[4] Recent scholarship has shed new light on the role that military studies played to educate British, American, and French Army officers prior to and during the War of American Independence, using books now in the possession of the Anderson House Library of the Society of the Cincinnati in Washington, D.C. The Society of the Cincinnati, founded by officers of the Continental Army, is the oldest patriotic organization in America. Its holdings include an extensive rare book collection from the American Revolutionary War period.[5]

Across Europe, the growth of military professionalism, which had begun in the sixteenth century, established the need for better-trained officers who could lead troops and effectively use the improved military technology that resulted from the introduction of gunpowder and "portable firearms."[6] Infantry tactics underwent significant change and infantry formations evolved from "lumbering dinosaurs ... massive squares of infantry made up of central blocks of pikemen fronted on all four sides by deep belts of musketeers," to infantry formations that deployed men in "shallower, linear formations" which allowed much more efficient use of the musket.[7]

The evolution of European armies did not occur in a vacuum. It evolved from the political, social, religious and technical change buffeting Europe, as the Protestant Reformation and the Enlightenment periods destabilized the previous medieval order of Western Europe. European governments evolved, in general becoming more centralized, autocratic and bureaucratic as they developed the administrative structures to fund and manage the state and the state-supported army. England was a bit of an anomaly, but its constitutional monarchy likewise developed an administrative structure to fund its military and to supply both the soldiers to staff it and the officers to lead it.[8]

England's journey toward military professionalism took a leap forward in the late sixteenth century as England re-engaged in the wars of mainland Europe. As early as 1572, Queen Elizabeth I (r. 1558-1603) sent military support to the Dutch Republic to aid that country in its struggles to be independent of Spain. Despite experience in England's internal wars, the English soldiers "found the new style of warfare in mainland Europe chaotic and bewildering."[9] Historian Roger B. Manning notes that the reintroduction of English officers to mainland European warfare allowed English officers to observe and gain experience in "new styles of command and standards of professionalism" as well as with the military tactics used by the Dutch.[10] Manning further notes that the Dutch innovations required much more of army officers; they were now responsible for "managing and training soldiers on a daily basis."[11] The new demands placed on officers encouraged them to address and improve their own skills. In this period prior to the existence of formal military academies, officers frequently turned to books to enhance their knowledge, for an "aristocratic military officer was expected to be well read and educated" and "[r]eading military treatises and memoirs was recommended as the best way to supplement the actual experience of battle."[12]

During the seventeenth century, English standing armies came into being, tied to the outbreak of the religious and dynastic civil wars that culminated in the rise of Oliver Cromwell and the New Model Army. The English Restoration period, which followed Cromwell's fall, not only restored the monarchy to England but it also reinforced the need to keep a tight rein on the army. It strengthened the English practice to limit the officer ranks to the aristocracy, a method thought to ensure the army's allegiance to the Crown and to the aristocratic order after the horrors of Cromwellian civil war.[13] The restored monarch, Charles II (r. 1660-1685) had limited options and financial means available to build an effective army. Thus, constrained by fears that a standing army supported despotic rule as well as limited by the financial wherewithal to support an army, the embryonic English professional army withered to a shell of its former self. Religious strife continued to plague England. With Charles' death, the crown passed to his brother, the more openly Catholic James II. James' Protestant subjects were frightened by the birth of a Stuart male heir in 1688 and soon "a group of English Protestants begged the Dutch Stadholder, William of Orange ... married to James II's eldest daughter, Mary ... to come to their aid."[14] By 1688, unable to withstand the invasion of William of Orange, the last Stuart king, James II fled the kingdom of England and the reign of his son-in-law began.

The concept of a military revolution in early modern Europe has been the subject of historical debate for half a century or more, beginning with theories espoused by historian Michael Roberts, who focused on the period spanning 1560 to 1660. Roberts's lecture, "The Military Revolution, 1560-1660," given at Queens University of Belfast in 1955, was critiqued by historian Geoffrey Parker in 1974 through an article titled "The 'Military Revolution,' 1560-1660—A Myth?" Parker challenged Roberts's assertions of a military revolution during the period in question as he analyzed earlier modes of warfare, particularly those of the Spanish and Italian armies, which preceded the innovations claimed by Roberts in areas of tactics, strategy, size of armies, and military theory. Historian Jeremy Black carried the argument forward in the twenty-first century. His article "Was there a Military Revolution in Early Modern Europe?" written in 2008, argued that Parker's assertions had limited applicability outside of Western Europe.[15]

Despite the on-going historiographical debate about the revolutionary nature of changes in early modern warfare and the origins of many of its defining elements, there is general agreement that the complexities of early modern warfare dictated the need for military books to provide insight and instruction to military officers of the period. Parker notes the emergence of illustrated military training manuals in 1607 with the release of "Jacob de Gheyn's *Wapenhandelinghe van roers, musquetten ende spies-sen* [Arms drill with arquebus, musket and pike]" which was published in Amsterdam and created under the supervision of Count John II of Nassau.[16] Parker further notes that this book was almost immediately "pirated and plagiarized;" and that it "rapidly [went] through numerous editions in Dutch, French, German, English, even Danish."[17] What were essentially military "textbooks" came into vogue early in the seventeenth century, enabling junior officers to train and drill their troops. Classical military treatises played a role in the advancement of military knowledge and techniques in the early modern period. Historian David Parrott notes that Dutch military reformers "stated explicitly that the basis of their tactical and organizational changes was a renewed study of the military prescriptions of classical authors – above all, Flavius Vegetius Renatus, Claudius Aelian and the Byzantine Emperor Leo VI."[18] Additionally, changes in the nature of fortifications and siege warfare, in response to improvements in artillery, brought about a new emphasis on learning mathematics, in particular for gaining "knowledge of trigonometry and logarithms" to construct the "*trace italienne*, a circuit of low, thick walls punctuated by quadrilateral bastions" which provided much better protection against bombardment.[19] Soon technical treatises followed — works on "artillery and fortification by French soldier-authors Vauban, Pagan, Belidor, and Clairac."[20] Perhaps the most famous of these authors was Sébastien Le Prestre de Vauban (1633-1707), of whom it has been said that he "established a nearly-infallible routine which was accessible to ordinary mortals who were willing to take the trouble to become versed in it."[21] A fortress built according to Vauban's specifications would withstand attack while a fortress besieged according to Vauban's methods was sure to fall.[22]

King Louis XIV (r. 1643-1715) has been credited with guiding France to become "[t]he leading military power and model for most of late seventeenth- century Europe." In doing so, France and Louis XIV profited from the ministries of Jean Baptiste Colbert (1619-1683) and of Michel Le Tellier (1603-1685) and his son, François

Michel Le Tellier (1641-1691). These men were instrumental in driving improvement to France's administrative and fiscal structure to better support France's military efforts. French administrative reforms "reduced the abuses and wastage which had undermined earlier French military efforts."[23] The war-like Louis XIV enlarged his dominions substantially and by the end of the French conflict with the Dutch through 1672-1679, had "made the largest territorial gains of the last 250 years of the French monarchy."[24] France's bold military expansionism, its absolute monarchy and its adherence to the hierarchical Roman Catholic faith set it at odds with the closely allied Protestant kingdom of England (Great Britain following the 1707 Act of Union) and the Dutch republic. Manning claims that the selection of William and Mary to rule England set in motion a period of warfare between Britain and France that lasted until the French Revolution and Napoleonic wars of the early nineteenth century. The wars between Britain and France came to encompass much of Europe as well as colonial North America, embroiling the colonists of both countries in a protracted struggle for control of America.[25]

Colonial America's experience with war differed remarkably from that of Britain and France. The European colonization of the New World created a collision of alien peoples. The European colonists and the indigenous peoples they encountered created an extraordinarily combustible mixture. The colonists saw the Native Americans as a truly alien race; that perception significantly affected how they waged war with the natives. English colonists brought their institutions, world-view, and prejudice with them as they crossed the Atlantic. One of their transplanted institutions was the English militia system. Their imported world-view included a deeply held Protestant faith and an abject hatred for their European rivals, the French "papists." In his analysis of the early "American Way of

War," historian Don Higginbotham outlined the state of the military historiography of colonial America and noted that the colonists adapted a type of total war in the colonies as they sought to annihilate their adversaries. While their European counterparts reacted with horror to the bloody Thirty Years' War and adopted a "more restrained" approach to warfare, the colonists felt that their very existence was at stake in the conflicts in the New World and fought with "a zeal for destroying their enemies."[26] Interestingly, Higginbotham postulates that there were various levels of the colonial way of war. He states that the colonists were most brutal to their Indian adversaries, more "restrained" toward their typical enemies, the French and Spanish, and most civilized toward their British cousins in the American War of Independence.[27]

How war was conducted during the American War of Independence was thus influenced not only by military trends developed over the preceding centuries in Europe but also by colonial Americans' experience gained in New World conflicts. Historians have debated whether the American Revolution was a radical rebellion or a conservative response to Britain's attempt to wrest increased revenue from the mainland colonies.[28] Regardless of the political nature of the rebellion, the choice of George Washington as Commander-in-Chief of the Continental Army, established the conservative Washington in command, rather than his chief rival, the radical Charles Lee. Had the Continental Congress elected to elevate Lee to top command, it is highly likely that the nature of war in the colonies would have been much different, as Lee espoused a reliance on irregular warfare, rather than the more conventional forms of warfare adopted by Washington.[29] While the rebels' colonial militia was to play a large role throughout the American War for Independence, Washington favored the development of a European-styled army.[30] Through his earlier experience in the French and Indian War, Washington developed an appreciation for the British practice of military study. As noted by historian Ira D. Gruber, "[b]ooks were essential to the eighteenth-century British army and its officer corps ... officers turned to ... books to expand their knowledge of wars and warfare ... to keep abreast of developments in the art of war [and] to share specialized knowledge."[31]

Gruber traces Britain's path to the development of a professional officer corps and standing army, noting the unique position of the British Isles to insulate England – and later Britain – from many of the military developments on the continent until, as earlier noted, England's involvement in the Dutch wars. Gruber states that the English Glorious Revolution, which brought William and Mary to the throne, was the turning point for England. With their ascension, the new monarchs and Parliament adopted measures to "impose taxes ... raise standing armies ... [and] create a permanent and responsible bureaucracy to manage those forces ... ensuring that soldiers were subordinate to the king in Parliament."[32] In part due to these developments, the British officer corps continued to advance in its professional progress, supported by on-the-job experience, a wide array of military reading material, and the establishment of the Royal Military Academy at Woolwich during the middle of the eighteenth century. The British academy at Woolwich specialized in training artillery and engineering officers who received an extensive education, primarily in various fields of mathematics. France created several military academies by the middle of the eighteenth century (the *Ecole militaire* in 1751, the artillery academy at La Fère in 1758, and several specialty schools which taught engineering) as did other European military powers, including Poland (the Polish Knights' School) and Austria (the *Theresianum*).[33]

Gruber's study of the military reading habits of forty-two senior British officers determined their preference for books devoted to "military and naval history, engineering, the art of war, and the classics" rather than books on "drill, discipline, and medicine" by the middle of the eighteenth century.[34] Gruber also noted that the British officers exhibited a strong preference for books written on the continent, especially those from France.[35] Similarly, a recent study on the reading habits of American and French officers during the American Revolutionary War by Sandra L. Powers, the Library Director Emerita of the Society of the Cincinnati in Washington, D.C., noted strong similarities between the books read by British officers and by French officers of the same period.[36]

Washington and his fledgling Continental Army were able to draw on a supply of well-developed military literature to supplement their limited military experience. While the privileged senior officers studied by Gruber shunned drill manuals, these books were necessary for the education and development of the Continental Army. Washington emphasized the use of military drill manuals to American officers. In a letter to Colonel William Woodford dated November 10, 1775, Washington counseled Woodford to study drill manuals:

> As to the manual exercise, the evolutions and manoeuvres (sic) of a regiment, with other knowledge necessary to the soldier, you will acquire them from those authors, who have treated upon these subjects, among whom Bland (the newest edition) stands foremost; also an Essay on the Art of War; Instructions for Officers, lately published at Philadelphia; the Partisan; Young; and others.[37]

In an early twentieth century analysis of George Washington's military studies, Oliver L. Spaulding, Jr. commented that the Bland military handbook was one of the most popular of its type in Britain during the mid-eighteenth century. Spaulding's personal review of the version that Washington had acquired found the Bland treatise to be "a most excellent statement of the art of war as known and practiced by Marlborough and his contemporaries, and as then practiced in the British army."[38] Washington, it seems, had been recommending Bland's treatise to others as early as 1756. However, the relative inexperience of the colonial militia and the soldiers of the Continental Army shaped the need for a simpler drill manual than Bland's. That manual dictated that soldiers follow "sixteen orders [and use] forty-nine motions to load their weapons.[39] Early in the war, an American, Captain Timothy Pickering, wrote *Easy Plan of Discipline for a Militia*, which streamlined the process. Historian Don Higginbotham noted that Pickering's *Easy Plan* reduced the number of movements to load a musket from forty-nine to ten and the officers' commands from sixteen orders to one. In addition, Pickering encouraged soldiers to aim their weapons — not a practice normally emphasized in the British ranks, which relied on a short-range discharge of massed musket fire for deadly effectiveness.[40]

The Continental Army also benefitted from a number of European "imports," notably Friedrich Wilhelm von Steuben, who became known as the "Drillmaster" of the American Revolution. Steuben's efforts were essential to develop the professionalism of the Continental Army, its officers and soldiers. Before Steuben's arrival, American officers had used whichever drill method they had learned, be it Prussian, French, or British. Steuben, working with the Continental Army at its winter quarters in Valley Forge, Pennsylvania during the winter of 1778, instilled a consistency of drill and maneuver for the army, enshrined in his *Regulations for the Order and Discipline of the Troops of the United States*, published in 1779. Historian Paul Lockhart notes that in the campaigns that followed Valley Forge, the "Continental Army demonstrated again and again that its metamorphosis at Valley Forge was no temporary phenomenon."[41] Steuben's students had learned their lessons well.

Technical books on artillery, fortification and siege warfare were important sources of military education during the eighteenth century. In addition to reading books, however, Washington benefitted from the expertise of several foreign military engineers, including Polish Colonel Thaddeus Kosciuszko who served the American cause throughout the war. Powers notes in her study of military books known to American officers that there was physical evidence of Americans' engineering studies. British officer Lachlan Campbell noted in his diary:

> The face of the country can only be compared to one of the demonstrative Plates of Treatises on Fortification when a number of plans are inscerted [sic] in an accidental Irregularity calculated only to make the most of the space. . . . The General designs of their works are Erected from Mons. Clairac's Elements de Fortification.[42]

While Kosciuszko has received acclaim from historians for his contributions to the American cause, in at least one instance he neglected to follow the structures of military science then in fashion and failed in his attempt to take an enemy fort. Kosciuszko, as an engineering advisor, accompanied Continental Army Major General Nathanael Greene to lay siege to the British outpost of Ninety Six, South Carolina in April 1781. Without following the formulaic approach to begin siege parallels at a significant distance from the targeted fortification, Kosciuszko and Greene instructed their men to dig their initial trenches within seventy feet of the fort. Their opponents, the British and Loyalist forces at Ninety Six were more conscientious in their preparations. Lieutenant Henry Haldane, a military engineer sent by Cornwallis to the post, designed one of the redoubts as a star fort, an eight-pointed design that allowed defenders to fire musket and cannon in all directions, following a seventeenth century innovation of Vauban's.[43] Cannon fire from the fort decimated the American sappers. "Their lesson quickly learned, the Americans began their next round of parallel siege trenches at a more respectful distance [400 yards]."[44]

Kosciuszko's lapse at Ninety Six was a minor mistake, however, and had no bearing on the outcome of the war. A much more famous siege occurred several months later at Yorktown, Virginia. Here the Americans and their French allies executed a classic eighteenth century siege, the result of which spelled the end of Britain's lengthy war to retain its mainland American colonies.

Despite a lack of formal military training available to his officers, Washington succeeded in creating an environment that encouraged learning. However, Americans did not simply adopt European methods, but integrated them into the Continental Army and American militias in such a way that reflected the strengths and weaknesses of American colonial culture. For instance, Steuben observed, "the genius of this nation is not in the least to be compared with that of the Prussians, Austrians, or French. You say to your soldier, 'Do this,' and he doeth it, but I am obliged to say, "This is the reason why you ought to do that,' and he does it."[45] Steuben realized that he needed to adjust his training methods to reach his American students; by doing so, his pupils at Valley Forge repaid his efforts and responded to his modified techniques. After Valley Forge, the Continental Army displayed its new-found capabilities at the Battle of Monmouth Courthouse, noted by Shy as a "soldiers' victory."[46] Following Steuben's training, the rank and file of the Continental Army were able to take the field and perform admirably in the face of the professional British forces. From military drill manuals that simplified and standardized military roles and maneuvers to training exercises which had been adapted to their needs, the American Continental Army learned to effectively fight and together with their

French allies, win America's independence.

Notes

[1] George Washington, General Orders, 8 May 1777," Founders Online, National Archives *The Papers of George Washington*, Revolutionary War Series, vol. 9, *28 March 1777–10 June 1777*, ed. Philander D. Chase. Charlottesville: University Press of Virginia, 1999. http://founders.archives.gov/documents/Washington/03-09-02-0356 (accessed September 4, 2013); Terry Golway, *Washington's General: Nathanael Greene and the Triumph of the American Revolution* (New York: Henry Holt and Company, LLC, 2005), 21, 29, 42, 54, 58.

[2] Fred Anderson, *Crucible of War: The Seven Years' War and the Fate of Empire in British North America, 1754-1766* (2000; repr., London: Faber and Faber, 2001), 92; Oliver L. Spaulding, Jr. "The Military Studies of George Washington," *The American Historical Review* 29, no. 4 (July 1924): 675-680. http://www.jstor.org/stable/1841231 (accessed September 5, 2013).

[3] Spaulding, Jr. "The Military Studies of George Washington," 676.

[4] Two recently published scholarly works which investigate the military works read by British, American, and French officers during the period leading up to and including the American Revolutionary War are Ira D. Gruber's *Books and the British Army in the Age of the American Revolution* (Chapel Hill: University of North Carolina Press, 2010); Sandra L. Powers, "Studying the Art of War: Military Books Known to American Officers and Their French Counterparts During the Second Half of the Eighteenth Century." *The Journal of Military History* 70 no. 3 (July 2006): 781-814. http://search.proquest.com.ezproxy2.apus.edu/docview/195628511?accountid=8289 (accessed September 4, 2013).

[5] "About the Society," *The Society of the Cincinnati* http://www.societyofthecincinnati.org/ (accessed November 11, 2013); "Collections Overview," *The Society of the Cincinnati,* http://www.societyofthecincinnati.org/collections (accessed November 11, 2013).

[6] Jeremy Black, "Was There a Military Revolution in Early Modern Europe?" *History Today* 58, no. 7 (July 2008): 35. http://search.proquest.com.ezproxy1.apus.edu/docview/202824124?accountid=8289 (accessed November 3, 2013).

[7] David Parrott, "The Military Revolution in Early Modern Europe," *History Today* 42 (Dec 1992): 21. http://search.proquest.com.ezproxy1.apus.edu/docview/202806562?accountid=8289 (accessed November 3, 2013).

[8] Ibid.

[9] Roger B. Manning, "Styles of Command in Seventeenth-Century English Armies," *The Journal of Military History* 71, no. 3 (July 2007): 672. http://search.proquest.com.ezproxy1.apus.edu/docview/195637168?accountid=8289 (accessed November 4, 2013).

[10] Ibid., 674.

[11] Ibid., 675.

[12] Ibid.

[13] Manning, "Styles of Command in Seventeenth-Century English Armies," 683; Micheál Ó Siochrú, "Ireland and the War of the Three Kingdoms," *BBC British*

History, (February 17, 2011) http://www.bbc.co.uk/history/british/
civil_war_revolution/ireland_kingdoms_01.shtml (accessed November 8, 2013).

[14] Mark Stoyle, "Overview: Civil War and Revolution, 1603 – 1714," *BBC British History* (February 17, 2011) http://www.bbc.co.uk/history/british/
civil_war_revolution/overview_civil_war_revolution_01.shtml (accessed November 8, 2013).

[15] Geoffrey Parker, "The 'Military Revolution,' 1560-1660—A Myth?" *The Journal of Modern History* 48, no. 2 (June 1976): 195. http://www.jstor.org/
stable/1879826 (accessed November 9, 2013); Black, "Was there a Military Revolution in Early Modern Europe?"

[16] Ibid., 202.

[17] Ibid.

[18] Ibid., 25.

[19] Parker, "The 'Military Revolution," 203; Manning, "Styles of Command in Seventeenth-Century English Armies," 675-676.

[20] Sandra L. Powers, "Studying the Art of War: Military Books Known to American Officers and Their French Counterparts During the Second Half of the Eighteenth Century," *The Journal of Military History* 70, no. 3 (July 2006): 783.

[21] Jamel M. Ostwald, *Vauban's Siege Legacy in The War of the Spanish Succession, 1702-1712*, PhD diss., The Ohio State University, 2002, 15. http://
etd.ohiolink.edu/send-pdf.cgi/Ostwald%20Jamel%20M.pdf?osu1039049324 (accessed November 10, 2013).

[22] Ostwald, *Vauban's Siege Legacy*, 16.

[23] Peter Wilson, "Warfare in the Old Regime 1648-1789," in *European Warfare 1453-1815*, ed. Jeremy Black (New York: Palgrave Macmillan, 1999)," 78; J. P. Sommerville, "Louis XIV and France," http://faculty.history.wisc.edu/
sommerville/351/351-13.htm (accessed November 9, 2013); "Jean-Baptiste Colbert," *Chateau de Versailles,* http://en.chateauversailles.fr/history/court-people/
louis-xiv-time/jean-baptiste-colbert (accessed November 9, 2013).

[24] Wilson, "Warfare in the Old Regime 1648-1789," 79.

[25] Manning, "Styles of Command in Seventeenth-Century English Armies," 684-685.

[26] Don Higginbotham, "The Early American Way of War: Reconnaissance and Appraisal," *The William and Mary Quarterly* 44, no. 2 (April 1987): 231. http://
personal.tcu.edu/gsmith/GraduateCourse/Colonial%20PDF%20Articles/
Higginbotham.pdf (accessed November 9, 2013).

[27] Ibid., 234.

[28] Gordon S. Wood, *The Radicalism of the American Revolution* (1991; repr., New York: Vintage Books, 1993), 3-8; John Shy, *A People Numerous & Armed: Reflection on the Military Struggle for American Independence* (1990; repr., Ann Arbor, MI: The University of Michigan Press, 1993), 161.

[29] Shy, *A People Numerous & Armed*, 138-140, 147.

[30] Jeremy Black, "Rethinking the Revolutionary War," *MHQ: The Quarterly Journal of Military History* 17, no. 3 (Spring 2005): 45. http://search.proquest.com.
ezproxy2.apus.edu/docview/223682517?accountid=8289 (accessed November 10, 2013).

31 Ira D. Gruber, *Books and the British Army in the Age of the American Revolution* (Chapel Hill, NC: The University of North Carolina Press, 2010),

32 Gruber, *Books and the British Army*, 22.

33 F. G. Guggisberg, *"The Shop:" The Story of the Royal Military Academy* (London: Cassell and Company, Limited. 1900), 1 http://archive.org/stream/shopstoryroyalm02gugggoog#page/n24/mode/2up (accessed September 21, 2013); Roy Porter, ed., *The Cambridge History of Science, Volume 4: Eighteenth-Century Science* (Cambridge: Cambridge University Press, 2003), 74.

34 Gruber, *Books and the British Army*, 11.

35 Ibid., 11-13.

36 Sandra L. Powers, "Studying the Art of War: Military Books Known to American Officers and Their French Counterparts During the Second Half of the Eighteenth Century," *The Journal of Military History* 70, no. 3 (July 2006): 787. http://search.proquest.com.ezproxy2.apus.edu/docview/195628511?accountid=8289 (accessed September 4, 2013).

37 "George Washington to Colonel William Woodford, 10 November 1775," Founders Online, National Archives (http://founders.archives.gov/documents/Washington/03-02-02-0320, ver. 2013-09-28). Source: *The Papers of George Washington*, Revolutionary War Series, vol. 2, *16 September 1775–31 December 1775*, ed. Philander D. Chase. Charlottesville: University Press of Virginia, 1987, pp. 346–347. (accessed November 10, 2013).

38 Spaulding, Jr., "The Military Studies of George Washington," 676.

39 Don Higginbotham, *The War of American Independence: Military Attitudes, Policies, and Practice, 1763-1789* (New York: The Macmillan Company, 1971), 47.

40 Higginbotham, *The War of American Independence*, 47; Spaulding, Jr., "The Military Studies of George Washington," 676.

41 Paul Lockhart, "Steuben Comes to America," *MHQ: The Quarterly Journal of Military History* 22, no. 2 (Winter 2010): 34. http://search.proquest.com.ezproxy1.apus.edu/docview/89238240?accountid=8289 (accessed November 10, 2013).

42 Powers, "Studying the Art of War," 793.

43 Burton Wright, "A Fenius for Fortification: Vauban and the Future of Positional Warfare," *Engineer* 30, no. 2 (April 2000): 37-39. http://search.proquest.com.ezproxy2.apus.edu/docview/196436729?accountid=8289 (accessed November 10, 2013).

44 Anne Midgley, "Ninety Six – Strategic Backcountry Outpost and Microcosm of the American Revolutionary War," *Saber and Scroll Journal* II, Issue I (Winter 2013): 25. http://saberandscroll.weebly.com/uploads/1/1/7/9/11798495/_journalv2i1.pdf

45 Robert Middlekauff, *The Glorious Cause: The American Revolution, 1763-1789* (Revised ed. New York: Oxford University Press, 2005), 425.

46 Shy, *A People Numerous & Armed*, 158.

Bibliography

"About the Society." *The Society of the Cincinnati.* http://www.societyofthecincinnati.org/ (accessed November 11, 2013).

Anderson, Fred. *Crucible of War: The Seven Years' War and the Fate of Empire in British North America, 1754-1766.* 2000. Reprint, London: Faber and Faber, 2001.

Black, Jeremy. "Rethinking the Revolutionary War." *MHQ: The Quarterly Journal of Military History* 17, no. 3 (Spring 2005): 42-51. http://search.proquest.com. ezproxy2.apus.edu/docview/223682517?accountid=8289 (accessed November 10, 2013).

_____. "Was There a Military Revolution in Early Modern Europe?" *HistoryToday* 58, no. 7 (July 2008). http://search.proquest.com.ezproxy2.apus.edu/ docview/202824124?accountid=8289 (accessed October 12, 2013).

"Collections Overview." *The Society of the Cincinnati.* http://www.societyofthecin-cinnati.org/collections (accessed November 11, 2013).

Ferling, John. *Almost a Miracle: The American Victory in the War of Independence.* New York: Oxford University Press, 2007.

Fischer, David Hackett. *Washington's Crossing.* New York: Oxford University Press, 2004.

Golway, Terry. *Washington's General: Nathanael Greene and the Triumph of the American Revolution.* New York: Henry Holt and Company, LLC, 2005.

Gruber, Ira D. *Books and the British Army in the Age of the American Revolution.* Chapel Hill: University of North Carolina Press, 2010.

Guggisberg, F. G. *"The Shop:" The Story of the Royal Military Academy.* London: Cassell and Company, Limited. 1900.

Higginbotham, Don. *The War of American Independence: Military Attitudes, Policies, and Practice, 1763-1789.* New York: The Macmillan Company, 1971.

_____. "The Early American Way of War: Reconnaissance and Appraisal," *The William and Mary Quarterly* 44, no. 2 (April 1987): 231. http://personal.tcu. edu/gsmith/GraduateCourse/Colonial%20PDF%20Articles/Higginbo-tham.pdf (accessed November 9, 2013).

"Jean-Baptiste Colbert," *Chateau de Versailles,* http://en.chateauversailles.fr/ history/court-people/louis-xiv-time/jean-baptiste-colbert (accessed November 9, 2013).

Lockhart, Paul. "Steuben Comes to America." *MHQ: The Quarterly Journal of Military History* 22, no. 2 (Winter 2010): 26-35,7. http://search.proquest.com. ezproxy1.apus.edu/docview/89238240?accountid=8289 (accessed November 10, 2013).

Manning, Roger B. "Styles of Command in Seventeenth-Century English Armies." *The Journal of Military History* 71, no. 3 (July 2007): 671-699. http://search.proquest.com.ezproxy1.apus.edu/docview/195637168?accountid=8289 (accessed November 4, 2013).

Middlekauff, Robert. *The Glorious Cause: The American Revolution, 1763-1789.* Revised ed. New York: Oxford University Press, 2005.

Midgley, Anne. "Ninety Six – Strategic Backcountry Outpost and Microcosm of the American Revolutionary War." *Saber and Scroll Journal* II, Issue I (Winter 2013): 25. http://saberandscroll.weebly.com/uploads/1/1/7/9/11798495/_journalv2i1.pdf

Ó Siochrú, Micheál ."Ireland and the War of the Three Kingdoms." *BBC British History.* (February 17, 2011). http://www.bbc.co.uk/history/british/civil_war_revolution/ireland_kingdoms_01.shtml (accessed November 8, 2013).

Ostwald, Jamel M. *Vauban's Siege Legacy in The War of the Spanish Succession, 1702-1712,* PhD diss., The Ohio State University, 2002. http://etd.ohiolink.edu/send-pdf.cgi/Ostwald%20Jamel%20M.pdf?osu1039049324 (accessed November 10, 2013).

Parker, Geoffrey. "The 'Military Revolution,' 1560-1660—A Myth?" The Journal of Modern History 48, no. 2 (June 1976): 195-241. http://www.jstor.org/stable/1879826 (accessed November 9, 2013).

Parrott, David. "The Military Revolution in Early Modern Europe." *History Today* 42 (Dec 1992): 21. http://search.proquest.com.ezproxy1.apus.edu/docview/202806562?accountid=8289 (accessed November 3, 2013).

Porter, Roy. ed. *The Cambridge History of Science, Volume 4: Eighteenth-Century Science.* Cambridge: Cambridge University Press, 2003.

Powers, Sandra L. "Studying the Art of War: Military Books Known to American Officers and Their French Counterparts During the Second Half of the Eighteenth Century." *The Journal of Military History* 70 no. 3 (July 2006): 781-814. http://search.proquest.com.ezproxy2.apus.edu/docview/195628511?accountid=8289 (accessed September 4, 2013).

Shy, John. *A People Numerous & Armed: Reflection on the Military Struggle for American Independence.* 1990. Reprint. Ann Arbor, MI: The University of Michigan Press, 1993.

Spaulding, Oliver L., Jr. "The Military Studies of George Washington." *The American Historical Review* 29, no. 4 (July 1924): 675-680. http://www.jstor.org/stable/1841231 (accessed September 5, 2013).

Sommerville, J. P. "Louis XIV and France," http://faculty.history.wisc.edu/sommerville/351/351-13.htm (accessed November 9, 2013).

Steuben, Friedrich von and François-Louis Teissèydre, *Regulations for the Order and Discipline of the Troops of the United States.* Philadelphia: Styner and Cist, 1779. http://memory.loc.gov/service/rbc/rbc0001/2006/2006batch30726/2006batch30726.pdf (accessed October 29, 2011).

Stoyle, Mark ."Overview: Civil War and Revolution, 1603 – 1714." *BBC British History* (February 17, 2011). http://www.bbc.co.uk/history/british/civil_war_revolution/overview_civil_war_revolution_01.shtml (accessed November 8, 2013).

Thacher, James. *A Military Journal During the American Revolutionary War, from 1775 to 1783; Describing Interesting Events and Transactions of this Period; with Numerous Historical Facts and Anecdotes, from the Original Manuscript.* Boston: Cottons & Barnard, 1827. http://archive.org/details/jamesthachermil00revorich (accessed September 4, 2013).

Washington, George. "General Orders, 8 May 1777," Founders Online, National Archives *The Papers of George Washington*, Revolutionary War Series, vol. 9, *28 March 1777–10 June 1777*, ed. Philander D. Chase. Charlottesville: University Press of Virginia, 1999. http://founders.archives.gov/documents/Washington/03-09-02-0356 (accessed September 4, 2013).

_____."From George Washington to Colonel William Woodford, 10 November 1775," Founders Online, National Archives. Source: *The Papers of George Washington*, Revolutionary War Series, vol. 2, *16 September 1775–31 December 1775*, ed. Philander D. Chase. Charlottesville: University Press of Virginia, 1987, pp. 346–347. http://founders.archives.gov/documents/Washington/03-02-02-0320 ver. 2013-09-28 (accessed November 10, 2013).

Wilson, Peter. "Warfare in the Old Regime 1648-1789." In *European Warfare1453-1815,* edited by Jeremy Black, 66-95. New York: Palgrave Macmillan, 1999.

Wright, Burton. "A Genius for Fortification: Vauban and the Future of Positional Warfare." *Engineer* 30, no. 2 (April 2000): 37-39. http://search.proquest.com.ezproxy2.apus.edu/docview/196436729?accountid=8289 (accessed November 10, 2013).

Wright, John W. "Notes on the Siege of Yorktown in 1781 with Special Reference to the Conduct of a Siege in the Eighteenth Century." *The William and Mary Quarterly* 12, no. 4 (October 1932): 229-250. http://www.jstor.org/stable/1923261 (accessed September 5, 2013).

_____. "Some Notes on the Continental Army." *The William and Mary Quarterly* 11, no. 2 (April 1931): 81-105. http://www.jstor.org/stable/1921003 (accessed September 16, 2013).

Wood, Gordon S. *The Radicalism of the American Revolution.*1991.Reprint. New York: Vintage Books, 1993.

A Paratrooper's Foresight: General James Gavin and the Health of the United States

Timothy T. Tutka

> First, we must be honest with ourselves, and clear thinking in our analysis of our failures and our successes.
>
> James M. Gavin, *War and Peace in the Space Age.*[1]

> ...the thinking of the younger generation of officers is critically contaminated by the veterans of past wars. Thus they frequently find themselves preparing feverishly to fight the last war better.
>
> — James M. Gavin[2]

On August 6, 1945, a date which marked the transformation of warfare around the globe, the first atomic bomb was dropped. Hovering above the Japanese city of Hiroshima, an American B-29 Superfortress droned. Its payload, a bomb with the fallacious moniker 'Little Boy' was prepared to be detonated over its target, the Aioi Bridge. The crew was only informed of the substance of their deadly cargo hours before it was to be dropped. The word 'atomic' crackled through the headsets, the first bomb of its kind. The crew of the *Enola Gay* recorded their experience of Little Boy's destructiveness. Author Peter Wyden writes in *Day One: Before Hiroshima and After* what was seen by the crew, "A column of smoke is rising fast. It has a fiery red core ... Fires are springing up everywhere... there are too many to count... Here it comes, the mushroom shape..."[3] With this detonation of the world's first atomic bomb, warfare within the parameters of the Second World War, both strategic and tactical were superseded. But the reliance on ever bigger bombs would lead the world to the brink of mutually assured destruction (MAD), a concept which only brought about a false sense of security.[4]

Due to the development of the atomic bomb, warfare in the twentieth century changed greatly, a fact that required the rethinking of strategy and tactics. The "bomb" was thought to be the ultimate weapon that could not be matched; however, the United States' monopoly on the "bomb" quickly disappeared as the Soviet Union had developed a bomb of their own only four years later. Time has forgotten a lone voice during the Cold War, General James Maurice Gavin, well known for his airborne exploits with the 82nd Airborne Division in the Second World War, but little has been written on his post-war writings. The health of the United States was at the center of Gen. James Gavin's thinking. His writings in the post-war years: *Airborne Warfare* (1947), *War and Peace in the Space Age* (1958) and *Crisis Now: Crisis in the Cities, Crisis in Vietnam, A Commitment to Change* (1968) exemplify his passion to lead America into the future on and off the battlefield. His thinking was not muddled in fighting the Second World War over again but on grasping the threat which was posed against the nation and harnessing technological skills which would propel the United States into a secure twenty-first century. The "bomb" did not provide the answer and only brought about a more frustrating form of limited warfare. The dispersement of forces was at the center of Gen. Gavin's thinking. Fast moving, mobile airborne forces were required. Military thought was not to be caught up in fighting the past war but instead on looking forward to how the next would be fought. Gen. Gavin continually expounded upon these facts, arguing that tomorrow's fight would be different than yesterday's victories or defeats.

The Second World War brought some of the best leaders to the top of the American leadership pool. General James Gavin was one of these men. "Jumpin' Jim" Gavin, as known by his men, led from the front with his M1 Garand rifle in hand. As the German Blitzkrieg cut through Europe, American military personnel read that impregnable fortresses such as that of Eben-Emael in Belgium were captured with little to no resistance. Eben-Emael was captured not by a moving ground envelopment but by a new form of attack; vertical envelopment by airborne forces. The United States lacked a cohesive airborne force. Captain Gavin (at the time) had a hand in the creation of America's airborne forces. "Gavin was soon pulled from C Company to airborne headquarters by Colonel Bill Lee [father of the American airborne], who put the talented young officer to work writing one of the first doctrinal manuals for this new form of warfare, *The Employment of Airborne Forces*," writes Ed Ruggero in *Combat Jump: The Young Men Who Led the Assault into Fortress Europe, July 1943*. Ruggero also wrote that, "...The officers in the Provisional Parachute Group put in long hours, working out the details of how such an organization should be equipped and how it should fight."[5] However, Gen. Gavin would not sit on the sidelines as he sought a place on the battlefield to put into practice the tactics he helped fashion. He would get his chance leading the 505th Parachute Infantry Regiment of the 82nd Airborne Division into Sicily known as Operation Husky in July 1943.[6] Colonel Gavin sent a written letter out to the regiment before the commencement of the jump into Sicily, of which the final paragraph reads, "The term 'American parachutist' has become synonymous with courage of high order. Let us carry the fight to the enemy and make the American Parachutist feared and respected through all his ranks. Attack violently. Destroy him wherever found. I know you will do your job."[7]

The drop on Sicily during Operation Husky was far from a success. Paratroopers of the 505th were scattered throughout the countryside, forming small groups that fought toward their objectives. The town of Gela, Sicily was the objective for Col. Gavin and his men but as he traversed Biazzo Ridge along the Acate River to the east of Gela he quickly realized the predicament that the Forty-fifth Division and the First Division faced as they landed on the beaches of Sicily. "A German force on the ridge could launch an attack against the flank of the Forty-fifth Division... the ridge would give them a commanding piece of terrain right in between two American positions..." writes Ruggero. The Herman Goering Panzer Division stood poised to take possession of this position. The fight on Biazzo Ridge pitted stubborn light infantry soldiers against a heavily armored crack German division. Ruggero continues, "Gavin... saw the ridge for what it was – a key piece of terrain in the unfolding battle, perhaps even critical for the whole invasion."[8] The ridge, if left unsecure, would have allowed the German panzers to isolate one division and destroy the other. The lightly armed paratroopers could do little against the armor of German tanks. Col. Gavin quickly brought mortars and howitzers into the battle to provide the needed respite against the German artillery and armor. Both sides grew exhausted by the intense fighting with the Germans gaining little. "Gavin knew that somewhere down past the vineyard, the German commander was probably reorganizing and coiling for a renewed attack on the ridge... Now was the time for the paratroopers to attack... Gavin was about to ask more of them," opines Ruggero.[9] Before the Germans could advance on the weary paratroopers, Col. Gavin pushed forward first. With the help of the Forty-fifth Division, the 505th PIR was able to push the veteran Herman Goering Division off Biazzo Ridge. Col. Gavin's resourcefulness helped prevent the outflanking of American infantry divisions that were landing on the beaches of Sicily. With the same insightfulness Gen. Gavin saw that the future of the United States rested on the shoulders of those who could plan for the future battlefield. For Gen. Gavin, the pen became mightier than the sword.

Gen. Gavin wanted his readers to clearly realize that America's isolated position within the world was diminished by the technology that existed during the Cold War. The technological leap that occurred in the twentieth century changed the way in which warfare could and would be fought. Gen. Gavin starkly wrote within his chapter "The Decade of Decision: 1955-1965" in *War and Peace in the Space Age*, "Now with the greater ranges and unprecedented fire power of nuclear weapons and the hyper-mobility of missiles and supersonic air vehicles, the area of the tactical battle has increased beyond anything even dreamed of in the past."[10] A war on the global scale in the technological age would encompass the whole world like the preceding wars had not. Missiles could provide the means of delivering nuclear weapons from one continent to another with ease. The jet engine provided the means of transporting men and materials faster and farther than that of the Second World War. Gen. Gavin provided an enlightening look at mobility, as in the nineteenth century it equated to roughly 6mph, World War Two 300mph and future 'Earth War'... 600mph.[11] The speed of movement had, and currently has, the potential to bring warfare to any part of the world in a matter of moments. The defense of the United States therefore concerned parts of the world that were never considered vital until after the Second World War. Author Kashid Khalidi writes in *Sowing Crisis: The Cold War and American Dominance in the Middle East*, "President Harry S. Truman's address of March 12, 1947... constituted the first time an American president had designated the Middle East as an area that was crucial to the national security interests of the United States."[12] Massive nuclear weapons were thought to be the perfect weapon that would solve the problem of the "Earth War" acting as a deterrent to foreign aggression, but at what cost?

As previously mentioned, America's monopoly on a nuclear arsenal was short lived. "For a time the atomic monopoly had offered us something of a bargain-basement defense policy," writes author David Halberstam in *The Fifties*.[13] As the 'Iron Curtain' descended over Europe, American supremacy on the battlefield was secure, for a short time, with the new wonder-weapon. However, with this weapon came many concessions that were not forward looking and were only stifling to America's new place as a world power. The swift demobilization of American forces in the post-war years of the mid 1940s and the slashing of the defense budget was not realistic in its foresight, especially with the continual threat of Soviet aggression. On September 3, 1949, American singular ownership of nuclear power was canceled.[14] The Soviet Union and the United States both harnessed the power of the atom. The struggle for supremacy and the threat of an all out holocaust of mankind was just beginning.

The threat of nuclear holocaust was, and is, still real. Gen. Gavin sought to set a sensible definition for warfare in the nuclear age and for the future as well. Warfare would not adhere to a flexible pendulum that would swing between war and peace during this period. Warfare would be constant. "I believe that by now most thoughtful people recognize as obsolete for our time this [Karl von Clausewitz's dictum of defined war and peace] simplistic view of peace and war as two distinct times in a nation's life. There is economic war, cold war, espionage, guerilla war, limited war, the war of ideas, etc.," opine the authors of *Crisis Now: Crisis in the Cities, Crisis in Vietnam, A Commitment to Change*, James Gavin and Arthur Hadley.[15] The nuclear bomb provided the mode to which a society could be rendered extinct within a short amount of time. Wars that may be limited in their means had the potential to escalate to full scale confrontations with other nuclear powers across the globe. The wholesale killing of large parts of humanity were not acceptable. Though the world had its "ultimate" weapon wars still would continue in limited form.

Gen. Gavin quickly grasped that the atomic bomb was not an "ultimate" weapon. He did not take the side of either those who advocated the 'complete' use of the bomb in the context of 'annihilation,' nor did he side with the anti-bomb protestors.[16] He was sensible with the new form of weapon which man now possessed and its inherent destructiveness. Man has prevailed over many technological innovations throughout the history of warfare from heavy cavalry to the invention of the machine gun and that of the strategic bomber. Nuclear weapons were no different. Authors T. Michael Booth and Duncan Spencer wrote in *Paratrooper: The Life of Gen. James M. Gavin*, "Gavin's reaction to the atom bomb was not to be swept away by it, but to face it through 'dispersion'… 'Never again may troops concentrate as they have in the past. For example, a buildup similar to that for the Normandy assault would suffer a most disastrous scorching if caught under an atomic bombing or missile attack… a defending force opposing such an attempt… would have to remain continuously dispersed."[17] Limited warfare proved to be the 'dispersed' means by which mankind could avoid nuclear holocaust.

Limited warfare set the tone of the nuclear age and the future. Escalation into a general war would engender the use of nuclear means to decide a conflict. Many leaders within the Pentagon were certain of this point and also advocated it. But others, such as Gen. Gavin, sought to keep warfare within limited constraints. In a second meeting for the *Council on Foreign Relations* entitled "Nuclear Weapons and Foreign Policy" on February 15, 1956 Gen. Gavin defined the use of limited warfare and a more mobile Army:

> General Gavin reported that experimental Army divisions such as the 101st are stressing hyper-mobility. The organizing priority is (1) air mobility, and (2)

sustained combat capability... After the break for dinner, General Gavin launched into a discussion of types of limited war. He suggested that wars are limited either in the amount of force brought to bear, by the percentage of a country's GNP devoted to pursuit of the war, or in terms of the geography of the area of combat. The greatest guarantee of expansion of a war is provided by the limits of geography... In terms of trying to limit a war the European scene presents the most problems, while isolated area like Indo China presents the fewest. An area like the Middle East, which is a perennial trouble spot, falls somewhere in between these two extremes, The Middle East, which is the land bridge to Eurasia and Africa presents a changing picture depending upon the time in the future that trouble might break out, for all the forces in that area are in a state of evolution.[18]

Limited wars allowed for a cost effective way of fighting a war, while at the same time avoiding an all out nuclear conflict. Gen. Gavin's understanding of dispersion was soundly joined with limited warfare.

Gen. Gavin insisted that the United States must stay focused on continually adapting forces to the future battlefield, insisting that America could not get caught fighting the wars of the past. "Organizations created to fight the last war better are not going to win the next," Gen. Gavin writes in *Airborne Warfare*, "Keeping foremost in our minds the functional purposes of our means of ground combat, these means must be developed and produced so that they can be delivered to the battlefield in sufficient quantity to gain the decision."[19] Throughout his writings, Gen. Gavin hammered away at the point of 'not fighting the past wars better' but developing and creating means to fight for the future. Therefore, it was inevitable that space was to be the next place of innovation for the United States.

The "space age" had come upon the world with the innovation of rocketry and its implementation within the Second World War. Rocketry had a farther reach than what man had first thought within the realm of science and warfare. His advocacy of innovations within differing space platforms helped propel American boundaries into space. "[Wernher] Von Braun excited Gavin with farsighted military ideas such as an artificial earth satellite and rockets that could reach the moon," writes T. Michael Booth and Duncan Spencer the authors of *Paratrooper: The Life of Gen. James M. Gavin*, "Gavin concluded that the army should back a missile that could both loft a satellite and give the army an awesome striking range of 1,000 to 1,500 miles… Gavin sold the idea to Ridgeway."[20] He was driven by the intelligence that the United States lagged behind the Soviets and if we should fall far behind them America could potentially lose a war that did not see a single shot fired. "And while our strength is ebbing [within the parameters of technological advancement] our obligations are increasing," writes Gen. Gavin.[21] With the innovation of satellites, guided missiles and the exploration of space the earth's breadth was shrunk. Our defense hinged upon our ability to interact with space before others gained supremacy over it. In a letter to then Senator John F. Kennedy, dated February 16, 1959 Gen. Gavin writes:

> I really think that it is very important that we realize that we must consider our efforts as one of the "Western World" and that we seek to integrate and bring together our best scientific and industrial thinking. At present time we are compartmented in many respects, both by country and by service within the armed forces of the many nations associated with us. On the other hand, the Soviets are integrated across the board thus, once a decision is made,

with significantly greater economy of resources, they can achieve far more. In the long run, we will only survive in this contest when through an integrated far-seeing effort we can regain the initiative and cause the Soviets to watch and follow us as a clue to the technical future in weapons systems. This is possible, but will take a greater effort, and a more integrated effort, than we are now making. At the rate things are now going, it does not take much vision to see that the decisions that will determine our future as an independent people will be made through the use and control of space. In the records, so far, the Soviets have demonstrated their superior leadership, both technical leadership and psychological leadership, in their exploitation of what they have accomplished.[22]

Space was central in his thinking of American defense and the NATO (North Atlantic Treaty Organization) countries. As can be seen throughout history the complexities of warfare expanded exponentially with the advancement of technology.

With warfare involving the swathe of the whole earth Gen. Gavin did not shy away from the complexities of warfare. The technological resources that influenced warfare were much more complex than those of the past. Gen. Gavin alluded to multiple technologies that were being developed in the 1950s and 1960s; intercontinental ballistic missiles (ICBMs), satellites, aerial drones, and computers were just a few examples of the complex platforms that were being created during Gen. Gavin's tenure in the military. He insisted that military tacticians will have severely complex problems that will need to be thoroughly researched and understood because of the growth of technology.[23]

Even today the public continues to misunderstand warfare and the implications that technology has had on it. Warfare has changed as the public's perception of warfare harkens back to the Second

World War. Gen. Gavin was far ahead of his time in understanding that warfare had transitioned. In *The Utility of Force: The Art of War in the Modern World* author General Rupert Smith wrote in 2007, "Nonetheless, war as cognitively known to most non-combatants, war as battle in a field between men and machinery, war as a massive deciding event in a dispute in international affairs: such war no longer exist."[24] Gen. Gavin understood that a misunderstanding of warfare could potentially have an adverse effect on the decisions of politicians and those that vote them into office. He wrote in 1958, "The economic, psychological and technical factors all weigh more heavily on the outcome of combat between nations than applied physical force itself."[25] The public's view of warfare is on the physical, rather than the other three applied factors which General Gavin speaks of and which General Smith highlights decades later.

For a strong defense of the nation to occur the nation within must be healthy. Gen. Gavin, an orphan in his youth, comprehended that the United States could not fulfill its exploration of space, innovations in technology, growth in education, advances in medicine and defense, all while trying to stay ahead of the Soviet Union without a healthy societal structure. Peter B. Levy quotes in *The Civil Rights Movement* from a "Report of the National Advisory Commission on Civil Disorders (1968)," "Violence cannot build a better society. Disruption and disorder nourish repression, not justice. They strike at the freedom of every citizen. The community cannot – it will not – tolerate coercion and mob rule. Violence and destruction must be ended – in the streets of the ghetto and in the lives of people. Segregation and poverty have created in the racial ghetto a destructive environment totally unknown to most white Americans."[26] With the race and anti-war riots occurring throughout the United States in major city centers, the country looked as though it was crumbling under the weight of the Cold War.[27]

The aging paratrooper foresaw the need for the revitalization of American cities being paramount in the protection of the nation, as one cannot protect from the outside while the inside is slowly deteriorating. "Unless we realize the size and nature of our problem, any answers we give will be too little and too late – and indeed quite irrelevant," writes Gen. Gavin in *Crisis Now* in 1968, "Violence will increase and the overall breakdown of our national life will follow as a scientific certainty."[28] America was in the throngs of a societal shift as minorities within American ghettos and urban environments sought recognition which was long due to them. The anti-war movement was winning over more of the population. In his conclusion for the chapter "The Human Environment – The City," he writes, "I want to abolish 'we' and 'they.' To have both white and black become 'we.' The 'we' of *e pluribus unum* (from the many, one). I wish to establish that unity we dreamed of when we wrote: 'We hold these truths to be self-evident: that all men are created equal...'"[29] The health of the nation rested on that 'all men are created equal.' If our nation did not adhere to this truth then the defense of the country from outside aggressors would have been stunted, a point that Gen. Gavin saw as central to the defense of our nation.

In conclusion, the foresight of General James Gavin provided the nation with a sound basis for defense for the future based on his insight that warfare had changed as soon as the atomic bomb over Hiroshima, Japan was detonated. The singular dependence on an atomic arsenal lasted for a short time until the Soviet Union created their own arsenal of deadly atomic weapons. The future looked bleak as 'mutually assured destruction' was on the lips of many in the United States and around the world. Gen. Gavin illustrated that warfare on a global scale could with ease touch every continent like never before seen in warfare of the past. The usage of a single nuclear weapon would only spell disaster for a large concentration of soldiers. Dispersion and mobility were required by Gen. Gavin to respond to the physical battlefield. Limited wars were considered the only means to keep the world from spiraling into a nuclear war, where there would be no winners. In this technological age the defense of the nation depended on our ability to look forward and see the battlefield of the future and most definitely not preparing to fight the last one better. With the space age coming to fruition in the 1950s and 1960s a new avenue of defense was seen in the heavens. The earth below could only be secure if the skies above were. Gen. Gavin saw this as a vital avenue for research. Rocketry would not only provide the means to secure Earth but also space. During this period it was evident that warfare was becoming very complex with the myriad of technology, mobility, highly volatile nuclear weapons and limited wars sprouting up throughout the world. Gen. Gavin understood explicitly that the public needed to understand that warfare had transitioned and physical engagement on the battlefield would intertwine with economic, psychological and technical factors, in many ways surmounting physical engagements. The whole of this defense rested on the health of the nation from within. The civil rights and anti-war movements stressed the foundation of the country. Gen. Gavin clearly asserted that no technological weapon or defense could protect the nation that was falling apart from the inside. Gen. Gavin's honest assessments of America's failures and successes helped propel it into the twenty-first century.

Notes

[1] James M. Gavin, *War and Peace in the Space Age* (New York: Harper & Brothers, 1958), 288.

[2] Ibid., 269.

[3] Peter Wyden, *Day One: Before Hiroshima and After* (New York: Simon and Schuster, 1984), 247.

[4] Ibid., 235-247.

[5] Ed Ruggero, *Combat Jump: The Young Men Who Led the Assault into Fortress Europe, July 1943* (New York: Harper Collins, 2003), 28-29.

[6] Ibid., 1.

[7] Ibid., 126.

[8] Ibid., 283.

[9] Ibid., 317.

[10] Gavin, *War and Peace in the Space Age*, 216-217.

[11] Ibid., 216-218.

[12] Rashid Khalidi, *Sowing Crisis: The Cold War and American Dominance in the Middle East* (Boston: Beacon Press, 2009), 40-41.

[13] David Halberstam, *The Fifties* (New York: Villard Books, 1993), 27.

[14] Ibid., 25.

[15] James M. Gavin and Arthur T. Hadley, *Crisis Now: Crisis in the Cities, Crisis in Vietnam, A Commitment to Change* 2nd Printing (New York: Random House, Inc., 1968), 25.

[16] T. Michael Booth and Duncan Spencer, *Paratrooper: The Life of Gen. James M. Gavin* (New York: Simon & Schuster, 1994), 326.

[17] Ibid., 326-327.

[18] The James M. Gavin Papers, Box 20, The U.S. Army Military History Institute, Carlisle Barracks, Pennsylvania.

[19] James M. Gavin, *Airborne Warfare* (Washington D.C.: Infantry Journal, 1947), 175.

[20] Booth and Spencer, 367.

[21] Gavin, *War and Peace in the Space Age*, 13.

[22] The James M. Gavin Papers, Box 26, the U.S. Army Military History Institute, Carlisle Barracks, Pennsylvania.

[23] Gavin, *War and Peace in the Space Age*, 226.

[24] Rupert Smith (General), *The Utility of Force: The Art of War in the Modern World* (New York: Knopf, 2007), 3.

[25] Gavin, *War and Peace in the Space Age*, 232.

[26] Peter B. Levy, *The Civil Rights Movements* (Westport: Greenwood, 1998), 194.

[27] Ibid., 3-35.

[28] Gavin, *Crisis Now*, 99.

[29] Ibid., 142.

Bibliography

Booth, T. Michael and Duncan Spencer. *Paratrooper: The Life of Gen. James M. Gavin*. New York: Simon & Schuster, 1994.

Gavin, James M. *Airborne Warfare*. Washington D.C.: Infantry Journal, 1947.

Gavin, James M. and Arthur T. Hadley. *Crisis Now: Crisis in the Cities, Crisis in Vietnam, A Commitment to Change* 2nd Printing. New York: Random House, Inc., 1968.

Gavin, James M. *War and Peace in the Space Age*. New York: Harper & Brothers, 1958.

Halberstam, David. *The Fifties*. New York: Villard Books, 1993.

Khalidi, Rashid. *Sowing Crisis: The Cold War and American Dominance in the Middle East*. Boston: Beacon Press, 2009.

Levy, Peter B. *The Civil Rights Movements*. Westport: Greenwood, 1998.

Ruggero, Ed. *Combat Jump: The Young Men Who Led the Assault into Fortress Europe, July 1943*. New York: Harper Collins, 2003.

Smith, General Rupert, *The Utility of Force: The Art of War in the Modern World*. New York: Knopf, 2007.

The James M. Gavin Papers. Box 20. The U.S. Army Military History Institute. Carlisle Barracks, Pennsylvania.

The James M. Gavin Papers. Box 26. The U.S. Army Military History Institute, Carlisle Barracks, Pennsylvania.

Wyden, Peter. *Day One: Before Hiroshima and After*. New York: Simon and Schuster, 1984.

John Jordan. *Warships After Washington: The Development of the Five Major Fleets 1922-1930*. Barnsley, South Yorkshire: Seaforth Publishing. 2011.

In *Warships After Washington*, historian John Jordan explores the 1922 Washington Naval Conference and its effect on the interwar development of the British, American, Japanese, French, and Italian navies. Jordan's book of eleven chapters is organized into three parts; the first deals with the state of the signatory navies on the eve of the conference in 1921, the second examines the conference itself, and the final part analyzes the development of the five fleets from the treaty's signing in 1922 until 1930. Jordan argues that these navies stood at a crossroads after World War One. None were enthusiastic about embarking on prohibitively expensive fleet expansions, least of all Great Britain, the world's premier naval power in 1918. The British, as Jordan shows, were keen during this period on not only maintaining their naval dominance, but also preserving their strained coffers, preferably by limiting the ability of up-and-comers like the United States and Japan from rapidly expanding and sparking a battleship arms race. Jordan argues that until 1921, where the Royal Navy led, others followed; this would all change after the Washington Conference (7).

The United States and Japan were indeed planning their own fleet expansion programs after the Great War. The former was nonetheless eager to limit expenditures on large warships, and it was ostensibly with this goal in mind that the US government invited the five major powers to Washington DC in 1921. The other, less publicized motivator for the conference was America's desire to isolate Japan by abrogating the Anglo-Japanese Alliance. At the time of the conference France and Italy were both regional powers with regional navies, the former as a great power in decline, the latter as a young nation on the rise. Both hoped to benefit from a naval arms treaty to modernize their own fleets while curbing the larger navies. France expected parity with Japan, while Italy desired parity with France, her emerging Mediterranean rival.

Jordan illustrates how the treaty was as groundbreaking as it was succinct. It set a quantitative and qualitative limit on capital ships, stymieing a prohibitively costly and potentially destabilizing arms race. Capital ship tonnage ratios for the five powers were established at 525,000 for Great Britain and the United States, 315,000 for Japan, and 175,000 for France and Italy. Aircraft carrier ratios were set at 315,000 for Great Britain and the United States, 81,000 for Japan, and 60,000 for Italy and France. Battleships were also limited to 35,000 tons individual displacement and 16-inch (bore diameter) main armament, while carriers were individually limited to 27,000 tons. Furthermore, the treaty stipulated a ten-year "battleship holiday" in which no new capital ships would be constructed. A qualitative (but not quantitative) limit was also extended to cruisers at 10,000 tons and 8-inch armament. As Jordan reveals, the resulting "treaty cruiser" would become a prolific warship in all five navies.

Jordan suggests that the United States was essentially the winner of the Washington Conference. The US attained capital ship parity with Great Britain, an end to the Anglo-Japanese Alliance and a financially unpopular naval program, and a curbing of the Japanese battle fleet at sixty percent of the United States' own strength. However, the conference did come at the cost of forward bases in the Western Pacific, which sealed the fate of the Philippines in the event of war. Regardless, with her tremendous industrial potential, the United States had every reason to look upon the post-treaty era with confidence; if any of her rivals were to renege on their treaty obligations, the US could (with the blessing of Congress) simply outproduce them.

Great Britain also emerged a winner of sorts, reducing naval expenses while preserving (for the time being) her naval superiority over potential rivals. However, Britain's long-term prospects in the wake of the treaty were hardly promising as later events would prove. But, this reviewer would argue, that British inability to expand the Royal Navy to the extent necessary to nullify rivals (as she had done in the Victorian era) was not a consequence of the Washington Treaty; it was due to her inexorable decline as a great power in the wake of World War One. In this regard, the treaty arguably prolonged Britain's naval supremacy by curbing not only her own expansion programs, but those of her potential rivals as well.

Imperial Japan, America's emerging rival, benefitted from the clause prohibiting US bases in the Western Pacific. Furthermore, her stipulated inferiority in capital ships (sixty percent of the US Navy) was hardly a genuine impediment as the United States, besides possessing a much larger industrial base for shipbuilding, had two oceans to police. Nevertheless, a militant "fleet faction" in the Japanese naval hierarchy viewed the conference's outcome with dismay. In the opinion of hard-liners like the naval commander Kato Kanji, only a seventy percent ratio vis-à-vis the US Navy would give the Imperial Japanese Navy (IJN) a fighting chance in the event of war (72). The years 1941-45 would clearly illustrate that the fleet faction's insistence on this symbolic ten percent increase was meaningless.

Italy was pleased with the outcome of the treaty. While the "big three" debated naval power in the Pacific, she was flattered by the offer of capital ship parity with France. Though inadvertently sparking a naval arms race between Italy and the French Third Republic, it enabled the former to aspire to the role she so keenly desired as a young, ambitious Mediterranean power. Due to her small and ageing battle line, Italy would also be permitted under the treaty to build up to 70,000 tons of capital ships during the battleship holiday.

France, however, was humiliated. Her delegates had come to Washington expecting naval parity with Japan; instead France (the world's second largest colonial empire in 1921) was lumped into the same category as Italy. Jordan shows how the treaty established ratios, not by world standing or colonial responsibilities, but by the size of the navies at the time of the conference, an approach obviously favoring countries like the United States. The *Marine Nationale* had stagnated during the Great War (when the army had been prioritized) and 1921 saw it at low ebb. In any event, it made little difference; Jordan illustrates how France could only afford to build seven of the twenty-one treaty cruisers she desired to maintain her great power pretensions (73). Furthermore, her priority during this time was not on battleships but on smaller vessel types, and like Italy, the treaty permitted France to modernize her battle fleet by constructing up to 70,000 tons during the battleship holiday.

The Washington Treaty, though drastically curtailing battleship construction, resulted in a heightened focus on cruiser, destroyer, submarine, and aircraft carrier development across all five fleets. The third part of the book, the heart and soul of Jordan's narrative, deals with these technical developments. The author explores the various modernization efforts made to the signatory battleship fleets, as vintage vessels were now expected to continue in service, barring viable replacements. The nations scrapped their oldest vessels, while extensively modernizing those that remained. This rejuvenation ensured that many of the battleships which would see action in World War Two were veterans of the first.

The Washington Conference had eliminated battleships as the cornerstone of post-treaty naval construction; therefore, attention turned to an entirely new monster pioneered by Great Britain—the treaty cruiser. All five navies would commission a number of these vessels, with Japanese cruisers being especially powerful, and many would go on to play prominent roles in World War Two. Lighter warship development also continued largely unabated, and flotilla craft such as destroyers, like the treaty cruisers, were "hot items" of the 1920s and 30s. France in particular commissioned a series of "super destroyers" whose size and power would earn their designations as light cruisers in allied service. The IJN also produced, with their "Special Type" fleet destroyers, an impressive flotilla force for the Pacific.

Another result of stunting the traditional "big-gun" battleship arm had been to spur navies into pursuing innovative technology alternatives. As Jordan indicates, submarine and aircraft carrier development is perhaps the best example of this trend. All five navies developed large submarine fleets of various types. Especially inventive were the "fleet" and "cruiser" designs of France and Japan. Furthermore, since the treaty no longer permitted a number of large battleship and battle cruiser designs, such as the Japanese *Akagi* and *Kaga* and the American *Lexington* and *Saratoga,* the countries converted their hulls to carriers. In short, the potent World War Two carrier forces of the United States and Japan owed their existence in large part to the Washington Treaty.

In conclusion, *Warships After Washington* is a valuable addition to the literature on interwar naval history. Jordan's keen insight provides the reader with a heightened appreciation for the political motivations and technical ramifications of the Washington Conference on 1920s and 30s naval development. The book illustrates how the conference was central to the development and doctrine of the interwar fleets that would ultimately face one another on the high seas in World War Two.

***

John Jordan is a recognized authority on 20th Century naval history. He began writing about the Soviet Navy in the 1970s, and after the collapse of the USSR shifted his attention to the interbellum French Navy. He has been the editor of *Warship* annual since 2005, and is the author of the books *French Battleships 1922-1956* and *French Cruisers 1922-1956*.

TORMOD ENGVIG

Robin Binckes. *The Great Trek Uncut-Escape from British Rule: The Boer Exodus from the Cape Colony, 1836*. Pinetown, South Africa: 30º South Publishers (Pty) Ltd., 2013.

The book *The Great Trek Uncut* by Robin Binckes covers the timeline of European and Boer colonization in South Africa from the year 1486 when the first Portuguese settler placed boots on the ground until 1852, when the Orange Free State and Transvaal Republics were officially established and given autonomy from British rule.

The author covers in great depth every major and transitional event surrounding the internal and external settlement of South Africa by peoples such as the Khoikhoi, Xhosa, Zulu, French, Dutch, and British populations. He also construes the cultural reasoning for Boer-Khoikhoi and Boer-Zulu interaction; for example, why the Dutch referred to the Khoikhoi as "Hottentot" meaning "stammerer" in Dutch (25). Other notable events Binckes mentions are circumstances such as the emancipation of slave labor in South Africa, which led to the Manifesto of the Emigrant Farmers, penned by Piet Retief in February 1836. Further, he talks at great length about the massacres near the Bloukrans River and other places which followed the Retief party's massacre in 1838. Finally, he spends a substantial amount of time on post-migration events of the region, such as the British annexation of the Boer areas and the subsequent independence for the Boer Republics.

In his writing, Binckes' main intent is to differ from the mostly rote historical texts which talk about the period and tell about the Boer Trek in a holistic manner. He does this by seeking to talk about the events through the emotions surrounding the mass exodus of Boers from the British-held South Africa to parts unknown. Simply put, in doing so, he uses emotion to drive the reader in a manner which belies the almost 700 page length book. As he states in his introduction, "The journey of the Voortrekkers belongs to all South Africans - Black, White, Coloured, and Indian. For too long, the story had been sanitized…" (18). Binckes utilizes a multi-faceted approach and perspective to tell about the Boer Trek, which differs from previous texts, as most of those were from the early-to-mid twentieth century and as such, were very biased toward the Boer side.

The author uses many primary sources to gain these angles, most notably six different diaries from people such as Johann Jakob Merklein, a German explorer who spent extensive time at the Cape of Good Hope during the Dutch settlement period; and Erasmus Smit, a religious leader of the Boers who saw many of the Trek's events. However, he also uses other works such as Archbishop Desmond Tutu's Foundation website to give further expressive background from the native African (Zulu and Xhosa) viewpoints.

Within the book, there are extensive maps (22) and illustrations (41) which support the book's flow and storytelling. The author uses the maps to show the Boers' migratory patterns, the battle formations used at Blood River and other places, and the final establishment of Boer footholds in South Africa. While the maps give a great frame of reference to the geography and historical acts, especially in the Natal area, the drawings and photographs themselves lend the true emotional impetus to Binckes' work. In fact, over a quarter of the photographs were taken by the author himself while standing at such storied locations as Blood River, Vegkop, and uM-gungundlovu (the Zulu Kingdom's capital during the reign of Din-gane). By doing so, he allows the reader to place him or herself in the center of those battles and understand some of the methodology used by those leaders. This only further lends to Binckes intent to make the story more personal.

By utilizing the photographs, Binckes fulfills two separate purposes. First with the landscape photos, he gives an appreciation of the perspective with which the Boer and Zulu leaders made their tactical decisions during battles. With the settler photographs and drawings, the reader gains an understanding of the austere conditions and the emotional aspects of the Boers' everyday lives as they moved out of the "oppressive" British rule into the unknown.

As compared with other texts about this brief historical period, this ranks as the most complete one published on the subject. Other texts centering on the Boer Trek cover mostly the pinnacle events only or give a heavy bias toward the Boer side. Although Binckes postulates on what differing people at that time would have said or thought during an event's occurrence, he does this in an extremely informed and thoughtful manner which does not degrade the historical facts, a risk so often seen when an author deduces on exact events or past emotions.

Although the author spends a great amount of time talking about the background issues and events leading up to the Boer Trek, these are shown as periphery to the work. In fact, almost three quarters of the book concentrate on the time period between 1820 and 1852, the years generally acknowledged as the time frame of the Boer Trek (also known by the name "Great Trek" in some historical circles). A further strength is that during each subplot, Binckes masterfully transitions the viewpoint between the varied parties in- volved, whether it is through the eyes of a Boer, Zulu, or Christian missionary. Arguably the best example of this is when he explains the contradictory reasons surrounding the Retief party's massacre in the Zulu capital on February 6, 1838. Earlier in the book, he talks about how most of the native conflicts were started due to stolen cattle, which ironically enough, is one of the reasons Dingane uses to justify his slaughter of Piet Retief's exploratory party (27, 367). He also hones in on the warning issued by the Christian missionary William Owen to some of the Voortrekkers regarding the Zulu treachery (366).

There are a couple of weaknesses inherent in the book, most notably the work's sheer length and the chapter subtitles used by the author. While the extreme length and detailed scope of the book are exceptional for one who is researching in depth on this historical series of events, it can be overwhelming for someone wanting to gain just a quick overview of the Boer Trek. To address the length, the author uses chapter titles and subtitles at the beginning of each chapter to ease searching issues; however, the manner in which it is done does not lend to a handy referencing within the chapter itself.

For a reader not very familiar with South African history, "The Great Trek: Uncut" is a solid work which one can use in gaining familiarization with that nation's events. As well, for the avid histori- an or student performing research on African history, this book is essential reading and would make an excellent centerpiece work in his or her library.

NORMAN HARVEY

Niklas Zetterling and Anders Frankson. *The Drive on Moscow 1941: Operation Taifun and Germany's First Great Crisis in World War II.* Havertown, PA: Casemate Publishers, 2012.

Let us face it – there always seems to be lots of new books churned out on the Russian Front of World War II. Many are well-intended but add little to this field of study. Others, while not contributing to the overall knowledge base, go off on what one might charitably say are ill-founded tangents. One must now wonder about this book with such a buildup. This reviewer has an entire shelf of books that cover this topic alone. However, those readers with a more than passing intellectual interest in the East Front of World War II will discover a somewhat fresh and enjoyable book with a focus that is slightly different than common for books of this genre.

The thesis advanced by the authors in a somewhat oblique manner is that had the *Wehrmacht* captured Moscow, the USSR would have capitulated, or at least been forced out of the war. Since Germany failed to achieve this critical objective, this then was the turning point of WW II. The reasoning behind their thesis is Hitler's own stated fears that the war must be decided before the U.S. fully mobilized its economy and entered the war. Part of their thesis fails simply because the Germans' failure at Moscow was less contingent upon the future U.S. efforts in Europe than their own economic failures. Adam Tolze's *Wages of Destruction* neatly lays out the economic failure in terms of inadequate wartime production in this critical period for the Third Reich. The U.S. was confronting Germany heavily economically by mid-1942 by Lend Lease with its shipments of high-octane fuel to the Soviet Air Force, waterproof telephone wire and radios – and trucks. The commitment of the U.S. to a strategic air offensive hurt Germany greatly in the air from mid-1943 onwards on the East Front, but all this is in the future.

The book is well-written. At times, the authors' English phrasing is slightly skewed. However, for a reader picking up his or her first book on Operation Taifun/Typhoon they could do substantially worse. The authors write lucidly without descending into grognard-type terminology. A huge plus of this book is the amount of time the authors spend on the battles of Mtsensk and Mozhaisk. That emphasis alone makes this a book that the jaded reader wants as these two battles are given short shrift in most accounts. The great overview of logistics makes this a perfect primer for future logisticians. The casual reader will pick up more from this book on the German logistical challenges than many other works. The book's primary weakness is too much orientation on the German drive and not enough focus on the Soviet efforts to deny them victory. As a cliché goes from the current war against Al-Qaeda, the enemy gets a vote too – and here the enemy "vote" is downplayed perhaps a little too much. In addition, they underscore the political and military infighting among the different German commanders.

It is a well-executed book that neatly fills in gaps even within this period of the war that have been less emphasized. There is a surprising amount of new material. Moreover, the thirty-seven pages of appendices are a worthy read onto themselves. The book is well and freshly illustrated with many new and previously unused photographs. Although the book is primarily written from a German perspective, albeit not as one-sided as say *Hitler Moves East*, it is well written, well proofed and covers the critical aspects in a manner sure to appeal to even the jaded East Front aficionado.

ROBERT SMITH

The Saber and Scroll is an Online University Historical Research Society affiliated with the American Public University School System. The purpose of this organization is the promotion of historical studies through the encouragement of academic research and the development of a rigorously edited online publication; the broadening of historical knowledge among the membership that includes social communications, topical discussions, historical lectures and the pursuit of other kindred activities in the interest of history; and service opportunities to the school and community. We strive to bring students, faculty, alumni, and historians-at-large together for intellectual and social exchanges, which promote and assist historical research and publication by our members.

Club Officers

Carrie-Ann Saigeon-Crunk, President

Lew Taylor, Interim Vice President

Kay O'Pry-Reynolds, Interim Secretary

Dr. Richard Hines, Faculty Advisory

AMU

American Public University System

APU

www.apus.edu

Featured Titles from Westphalia Press

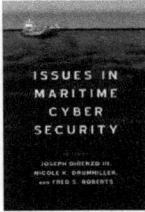

Issues in Maritime Cyber Security Edited by Nicole K. Drumhiller, Fred S. Roberts, Joseph DiRenzo III and Fred S. Roberts

While there is literature about the maritime transportation system, and about cyber security, to date there is very little literature on this converging area. This pioneering book is beneficial to a variety of audiences looking at risk analysis, national security, cyber threats, or maritime policy.

The Death Penalty in the Caribbean: Perspectives from the Police Edited by Wendell C. Wallace PhD

Two controversial topics, policing and the death penalty, are skillfully interwoven into one book in order to respond to this lacuna in the region. The book carries you through a disparate range of emotions, thoughts, frustrations, successes and views as espoused by police leaders throughout the Caribbean

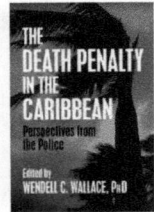

Middle East Reviews: Second Edition
Edited by Mohammed M. Aman PhD and Mary Jo Aman MLIS

The book brings together reviews of books published on the Middle East and North Africa. It is a valuable addition to Middle East literature, and will provide an informative read for experts and non-experts on the MENA countries.

Unworkable Conservatism: Small Government, Freemarkets, and Impracticality by Max J. Skidmore

Unworkable Conservatism looks at what passes these days for "conservative" principles—small government, low taxes, minimal regulation—and demonstrates that they are not feasible under modern conditions.

The Politics of Impeachment
Edited by Margaret Tseng

This edited volume addresses the increased political nature of impeachment. It is meant to be a wide overview of impeachment on the federal and state level, including: the politics of bringing impeachment articles forward, the politicized impeachment proceedings, the political nature of how one conducts oneself during the proceedings and the political fallout afterwards.

Demand the Impossible: Essays in History as Activism
Edited by Nathan Wuertenberg and William Horne

Demand the Impossible asks scholars what they can do to help solve present-day crises. The twelve essays in this volume draw inspiration from present-day activists. They examine the role of history in shaping ongoing debates over monuments, racism, clean energy, health care, poverty, and the Democratic Party.

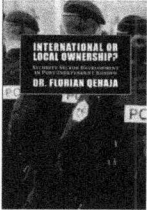

International or Local Ownership?: Security Sector
Development in Post-Independent Kosovo
by Dr. Florian Qehaja

International or Local Ownership? contributes to the debate on the concept of local ownership in post-conflict settings, and discussions on international relations, peacebuilding, security and development studies.

Donald J. Trump's Presidency: International Perspectives
Edited by John Dixon and Max J. Skidmore

President Donald J. Trump's foreign policy rhetoric and actions become more understandable by reference to his personality traits, his worldview, and his view of the world. As such, his foreign policy emphasis was on American isolationism and economic nationalism.

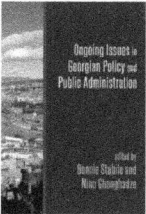

Ongoing Issues in Georgian Policy and Public Administration
Edited by Bonnie Stabile and Nino Ghonghadze

Thriving democracy and representative government depend upon a well functioning civil service, rich civic life and economic success. Georgia has been considered a top performer among countries in South Eastern Europe seeking to establish themselves in the post-Soviet era.

Poverty in America: Urban and Rural Inequality and
Deprivation in the 21st Century
Edited by Max J. Skidmore

Poverty in America too often goes unnoticed, and disregarded. This perhaps results from America's general level of prosperity along with a fairly widespread notion that conditions inevitably are better in the USA than elsewhere. Political rhetoric frequently enforces such an erroneous notion.

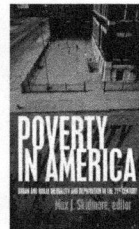

westphaliapress.org

www.ingramcontent.com/pod-product-compliance
Lightning Source LLC
Chambersburg PA
CBHW030106070426
42448CB00037B/987